FOREWORD BY
COREY RUSSELL

BEHOLDING & BECOMING

AWAKENING THE GROAN FOR GOD AND HIS PURPOSES

MICHAEL DOW

BURNING ONES
PUBLISHING

Bible quotations are taken from:

The Berean Bible (www.Berean.Bible) Berean Study Bible (BSB) © 2016, 2020 by Bible Hub and Berean.Bible. Used by Permission. All rights Reserved.

The *Holy Bible*, New Living Translation (NLT). Copyright © 1996, 2004, 2015 by Tyndale House Foundation. Used by permission of Tyndale House Publishers, Inc., Carol Stream, Illinois 60188. All rights reserved.

New American Standard Bible® (NASB). Copyright © 1960, 1971, 1977, 1995, 2020 by The Lockman Foundation. All rights reserved.

New American Standard Bible 1995 (NASB1995). New American Standard Bible®, Copyright © 1960, 1971, 1977, 1995 by The Lockman Foundation. All rights reserved.

The New King James Version® (NKJV). Copyright © 1982 by Thomas Nelson. Used by permission. All rights reserved.

DEDICATION

I dedicate this book to the people that love God's Son, Jesus, above all things. The people that long for Jesus to have His inheritance, and they want Him to have it in them. This book is for the fiery laid-down lovers that have abandoned all other dreams because He Himself has become the dream of their hearts and the ultimate obsession of their lives.

This book is for those whose soul sings, "Take the world but give me Jesus!"

There is only One worthy of giving it all for. There is only One worth living for, and only One worth dying for. The man Jesus, the bridegroom King, the crucified God. He is everything.

This book is for the wild ones, those who will ready the earth for the return of King Jesus. He is coming again. Our hearts burn for His coming. We hasten the day of His coming. There is a painful ache within that can only be fully satisfied in one way—We must have Him, and He must have what He wants.

Until He gets it, we groan. We groan together.

This is for those who groan. For those to whom God will awaken the groan within. A groan for Him and His purposes as we behold the beauty of His Son.

TABLE OF CONTENTS

ACKNOWLEDGMENTS

To my beautiful wife and best friend, Anna, and our five amazing children: Ariyah, Josiah, Emma, Isaiah, and Elijah. I love you with all my heart. I cannot thank you enough for the way you champion what God has done and is doing in my heart and life. Thank you for being my biggest fans. Thank you for the loving support and needed challenge that you contribute to God's purposes in and for me.

Thank you to our church family, The Father's House Orlando. Your jealousy to pursue what God wants in us as a people and in our city has helped to fuel the groan of God within me. It is an honor to share our lives together as we labor by His Spirit to build His house. Revival and the return of the Lord!

Thank you to our Burning Ones team. I truly believe we are the dream team. Grateful to have the privilege to lead such a precious and powerful group of Jesus lovers. Your love and faithfulness to the Lord and others have marked my heart.

Thank you to Kathy Curtis. It has been a tremendous joy to work with you over the years on all the books that I have been privileged to write. Your countless hours invested and excellence in editing has helped to bring these projects to life. You are a gem, and I honor you.

Thank you to my friend, my dear brother, Omar Galarza, for a cover design that absolutely hit the mark. You are a gift, and I am grateful for your contribution in this project.

FOREWORD

I'm convinced the Holy Spirit is delivering the church from a "me-centered" gospel where Jesus is all about fulfilling our destiny and our story and He is bringing us into something deeper, more profound, and more fulfilling; and it's Him connecting us to His story and His calling. As I read the Scriptures, beginning in Genesis all the way to Revelation, I see a glorious plan of redemption that culminates with the literal return of Jesus and the descent of heaven to the earth where the two become one. I believe that God is awakening this generation to this deep longing in His heart and a groan is coming forth.

Romans 8 points us to this groan as we join creation and God Himself in laboring for the fulfillment of everything hidden in His heart. This is why I'm so excited for Michael Dow's new book, *Beholding and Becoming: Awakening the Groan for God and His Purposes*. In this book, Michael gives a clear vision of God's heart and purposes and then calls us into joining Him in seeing the fullness of it released in our generation. I wholeheartedly endorse this book and even more this author. I believe this book is going to be the first in many to come that will shift us from me to Him.

Corey Russell
Author and Speaker

INTRODUCTION

Life is filled with longing. There is an ache in the human heart. This ache has a wild way of demanding satisfaction. Man has searched the world over in a myriad of ways in attempt to satisfy this yearning. The world recognizes there is a longing in the human experience and tells us how to go about satisfying it. Money. Power. Success. Influence. Fame. Prestige. Possessions. Sex. Drugs. Entertainment. Extracurricular activities. Hobbies. All the above and more are an attempt to fill the gap from within that cries out. Man pursues these paths because the world has told us these are the ways to get the job done. The world pushes to these spaces to try and pacify or satisfy this sense of longing within.

There is a groaning from deep within man's life and it attempts to create his course. This groan fuels his pursuits. Groan can be defined as a mournful sound uttered in pain or grief. It carries the idea of making a deep inarticulate sound expressive of derision, disapproval, desire, etc. It is a deep grating or

creaking sound due to a sudden or continued overbur-
dening, as with a great weight. To summarize these for
the sake of being concise, a groan is the expression of
an inarticulate sound due to

The Spirit empowers a radical aligning to God's desires.

mourning, or a continued painful burdening.

For those who are of the world, this groan comes
from unsatisfied appetites that are hungering. These
appetites usually get satisfied by the things of this life,
the things of this life meaning the things of the world.
This is where the difference lies for those who bear
God's Spirit. Those who have been born again from
above now house the precious and powerful Holy
Spirit. This reality has absolutely changed the game in
every possible way for the human experience in relationship to groaning and longing.[1]

Those who bear the Spirit do not hunger for the
same things the world is after. No, this should not be.
The Spirit has brought the much-needed transforma-
tion to our desires. We are now able to discern what
God wants, and by the Spirit, we can want it too. The
Spirit empowers a radical aligning to God's desires.
Our appetite has now been realigned to hunger after

---

[1] See John 3:3-8

what it is that we know God wants—to see His purposes fulfilled.

There is something that God wants. It has set everything into motion. In fact, what God has done is all connected to what He wants. Putting the fullness of who He is into Jesus, the wisdom of His cross, the shedding of His blood, raising Him from the dead, and having Him ascend to His right hand, and now the sending of the Spirit to be housed within those who repent and are born again, is all unto what it is that God is after.

All of what we just referenced fits into a beautiful story God has been superintending now for thousands of years. None of it is random. It is all aimed at a particular destination God is jealous for. He desires a predetermined conclusion, and all of time and creation are heading towards it.

Nothing can stop what God is doing. Not the enemy and his desires. Not the unleashing of demonic agenda by powers and principalities. Not the situation of evil, nor the rebellious nature of man and his desire to consistently want his own way and rule over his own life. Any and all perceived hindrances to the dream God has in His heart for creation and humanity have been conquered. The Man Jesus, He has overcome. Now men can be reconciled to God, and in that, also be reconciled to His will.

All who call upon the name of the Lord shall be saved.[2] To these precious ones He promises to fill. He fills them because He knows it is this born-again experience and filling that provide Him with the way He needs to transform them. God has sent His Spirit to fill humans, which will produce the work in them to ready them for what He has prepared for those who love Him.[3]

Being filled with the Spirit has awakened our hearts to God's longing.

Part of the work the Holy Spirit is doing in those who are born again is to jar them from the world and produce a different lens through which all of life now must be interpreted. The down payment of the Holy Spirit into the life of the one who has given himself to Jesus is what has altered our previous course.[4]

The traction with the world and all its attempts to satisfy the groaning from within will no longer do. We can no longer find our successes and our satisfactions in where the world points for them to be found. And the reason why is this—even if I had everything I think I want, there is still something I know God wants, and He doesn't have it in full yet.

---

[2] Rom 10:13
[3] 1 Cor 2:9
[4] See Eph 1:14; Rom 5:5

Being filled with the Spirit has awakened our hearts to God's longing. Out of the awareness of God's longing we experience a sense of mourning. We mourn because we understand that the human condition and creation itself are not enjoying the fullness of what God originally intended. We are not living in what it is God wants, and this tension has created a discomfort.

This mourning, this burdening, has awakened a groan on the inside. This groan comes out of a place where we know what God wants and we want it too. We want it too because His life has filled us, and it is producing His desires within us. The Holy Spirit both awakens and sustains this groan within.

The Holy Spirit is awakening the groan for God and His purposes. Deep is calling out to deep. A violent stirring is happening on the inside and it is making provision for a shift. The shift is to come out. The shift is to be separate. The time for being wholly swallowed up in the things of the world is over.

The shift is severing all lesser lovers and other attachments to life that have been used to create resistance from an absolute yielding to what God wants. There is something that God wants. Knowledge of it alone is not enough. We must yield; we must be completely given over.

God is touching the hearts and lives of those who love His Son and causing them to groan. We groan because we mourn. We mourn because we understand the crucible of the age. We long for God to reconcile all things as He has promised. We carry an ache within that can only be satisfied by God Himself and His purposes being realized. The Holy Spirit is awakening a people and they are being overtaken by the groaning.

God is touching the hearts and lives of those who love His Son and causing them to groan.

This groan is awakened on the inside, but it doesn't only affect things happening on the inside of us; it also affects everything happening on the outside. The groan affects how we set our lives up. There are a people who are setting their life up in response to the groaning the Holy Spirit is churning within them.

Jesus said, "Blessed are those who mourn, for they shall be comforted."[5] This reference to mourning is not just a group of people who live their lives being sad all the time. The idea is much deeper than that. It is a people who carry a sorrow. Their sorrow is from the great disappointment of knowing what it is that God wants, what He is after, and the distance we live in by

[5] Matt 5:4, NKJV

way of experience from the fullness of that reality. It is a people who, by the Spirit, have a capacity to house God's burden.

Housing God's burden and the tension that fills the human life when doing so produces a painful ache on the inside. This painful ache is the realization of what is on God's heart—what He wants—and all of what is currently set up to oppose and press towards other desires. The sin-saturated system of the age. The brokenness of humanity. Spiritual powers and forces of evil. There is much that is not right, much to disapprove of. Therefore there is a groaning.

This groaning will come to an end. God will come. He will fulfill what He has promised. He will make right everything that is not right. He will wipe every tear away. He will abolish death forever. He will be amid His people, forever.[6] He will have the family He has always desired, the people to share Himself with forever. This is what God is working all things together toward. It is His plan, His dream.

There are a people who are emerging that are coming into the revelation of what it is God is after. They are no longer deceived by all the world's enticements and the enemy's lures to find their fulfillment in other means. They are gaining clear sight of what

---

[6] Rev 21:3-4

God's dream is and they are giving the whole of their lives to it.

They are living out of the groan for God and His purposes rather than the groan for the world and the momentary pleasures it may offer. This world is not the place where they are seeking their greatest reward. They know the Son of Man will come riding upon the cloud, His reward with Him.[7]

A people are emerging because it is what God wants. God wants a people. He has gone to extraordinary lengths to have what He is after. He has made a way. He has created the path Himself. He has provided all the means necessary for the powerful people that He desires to be possible. He will have them. He will conform them into the image of His Son. They will rule alongside of Jesus as the bride He is deserving of.

Until He gets everything He wants the groan will continue. It will fill the hearts and lives of a lovesick bride. It will be housed in those who have forsaken all other lovers. It will churn deep within those who have caught a glimpse and been granted a taste.[8] It will rise within the wild ones; a people that will seem wild because they will not conform to the world and its ways.

---

[7] Matt 16:27
[8] See Ps 34:8

They will seem wild because their power source will not be of the world. They will not be powerful the way that the world defines powerful people. They will find God for themselves. They will live undone by His touch. They will give everything to Him and for Him. They will live for His reward. This will make them different. This will make them separate. Their purity will make them powerful.

God wants a people that look like His Son and love Him above all things.

God wants a people that look like His Son and love Him above all things. A people that will be so deeply connected to His heart and the things He desires that He can use them to help ready the earth for the second coming of His Son. They will house His groan until He comes for them. The groan will fuel their consecration to God. The groan will fuel participation in His purposes. The groan will fuel their anticipation of things He has promised.

This book will be a journey into beholding Jesus and becoming more like Him, and in doing so, having our lives completely wrecked by the awakening of the groan within for God and His purposes to be realized. May we never be the same.

CHAPTER ONE

SIN, STANDARDS, AND SUBJECTION

God has done the unimaginable. He has done what was previously thought to be inconceivable. He has become a man. God has taken on human flesh. In humility, He has become one of the creatures He Himself has created. The infinite has become an infant. God has entered the human story—not just as something that was above us or materially much better than us. He has come as one of us. He has come into the human story as one of us to do on behalf of us what none of us would ever be able to accomplish for the rest of us.

God planted Himself in the human story. He put the fullness of who He is into a man.[9] God sowed His own life into the womb of a virgin woman named

---

[9] Col 1:19

Mary. Her intimate surrender created a doorway for God's purposes to come alive in the womb of destiny.[10] That's usually the way it works. Lovingly yielding to God in joy-filled surrender bears fruit and births God's desires into the human experience.

> **Lovingly yielding to God in joy-filled surrender bears fruit and births God's desires into the human experience.**

The God-man would be born, Jesus the Son. He would go on to live the life no other man ever could— sinless, perfect. He willingly laid His life down, making atonement as the unblemished sacrifice for sin. He is the Lamb that was slain before the foundation of the world.[11] In this God has triumphed over evil and every objection to His dream through the laying down of His own life. Jesus, He has overcome. This changes everything.

What God has done has radically changed the trajectory of the human story. The chasm of sin had seemed to, at least for a time, derail God's desires for creation and those whom He had created. The enemy thought he had both formed and executed the perfect plan. He manipulated Adam and Eve in the garden

[10] Luke 1:26-38
[11] John 10:18; Ps 40:8; Heb 5:7-9, 12:2; Rev 5:12, 13:8

and got them to willingly bring compromise to God's desires.

They knew what God had said. They chose against it. Giving way to the enemy's influence they compromised the boundaries of the Garden of Eden. Sin entered the human story. God would banish them from the garden.[12] An inheritance fell on all mankind.[13] If you are familiar with the story at all, at this point all seemed to be darkened and derailed.

What was it about the plan the enemy put together that seemed to be so masterful? Great question. We must consider what the enemy was after when he led Eve to eat of the tree. We minimize and trivialize sin so often we don't truly understand the intention of what it is looking to produce in us or the trajectory that it longs to align our lives with. The issue that took place in the garden was no small thing. In fact, it seemed to affect everything for a time being, and in some ways it still has drastic effects on everything.

What God has done has radically changed the trajectory of the human story.

We are told that the wage of sin is death.[14] Meaning the ultimate penalty for sin, regardless of how much it

---

[12] See Gen 3
[13] Rom 5:12
[14] Rom 6:23

3

promises to satisfy you in the moment, is death. The real consequence for living your life in sin, regardless of what it seems to create in an immediate way, is that it leads to death. Death in an ultimate sense is very different than the human experience of death, which is what we most times think of. We think more immediate; someone dies, and they are not here any longer.

Death ultimately is a much more severe consequence than death immediately.

Death ultimately is a much more severe consequence than death immediately. Every man will die. The Bible is very clear that it is appointed unto every man a time to die.[15] However, it is what we are faced with when we open our eyes in the place of eternity that the wage of sin creates a disconnect from.

Sin wants to synchronize your life with a trajectory that derails you from what has been prepared for you in the place where what is ultimate will be realized. God has a dream for His creation. The enemy despises God and His desires. He hopes to successfully sever the connection you have to God and His plans through your engagement of sin.

The wages of sin desires to secure an eternal fate for you. Therefore sin must be seen clearly and its motives

---

[15] Heb 9:27

must be discerned rightly. The wages of sin has an ultimate concern of separating you from God forever. It is very serious because it is very true.

The enemy was not just interested in getting Adam and Eve removed from the garden. He was after the inheritance that would fall onto all of humanity through the efforts of Adam to remove them from the conclusion God had determined for them when He created them.

The enemy did not ask them to become one of his subjects. He didn't invite them to follow him. His offering wasn't one of him against God. This was never the plan. His plan was much different. He offered Adam and Eve the choice of following themselves, their own desires, instead of lovingly remaining subject to what they knew God had commanded. It wasn't the choice of choosing the devil's side; it was choosing what they thought was best or wanted.

The devil doesn't ask you to choose him; he asks you to choose you. In your choice of yourself above God you become like him without him asking you to do so. Remember, he is the self-exalted one who loves himself more than God.[16] Herein we find the essence of sin: a rebelling from God through the avenue of self.

---

[16] Isa 14:13-14; Eze 28:17

This is the plan the enemy launched and with it the plan to have humans conform to his way. They chose the enemy's way by choosing their own way and therefore rejected God's way, rebelling intentionally and entering sin. Even though

We must know what God wants so we can want it too.

they chose a deviation from the plan, God's plan was still at work.

God has a plan. He has a will. There is an eternal purpose for which God is working all things.[17] To say it another way, God has a dream. There is something He wants. It is important we identify and understand that God wants something. There is something very specific He is after. Do you know what God wants? Do you know what He is after?

God wants a family. God longs for a people He can share Himself with forever in the place of eternity. You could say it this way: God is a family man. I can say that God is a family man because God, in Himself, is family. He is a divine community, a family. Father, Son, and Spirit—the Trinity is a family-fellowship experience. And this family God wants is not something secondary to Him. It is the whole reason humans were formed: to lovingly enjoy God and rule alongside

---

[17] Eph 3:11; Col 1:9

of His Son forever as His comparable companion in creation. This is a big deal.

We must know what God wants so we can want it too. The Holy Spirit is working throughout the world to produce a people that want what God wants. If this is not understood, then much of our life experience cannot be interpreted rightly or lived out correctly.

We too easily create our own context and desired conclusions and then feel disappointed with God when He is not after what we want. We dream up our own dreams. We create a list of demands for the life we believe would be best for us. We have all our own ideas as to what would be the most fulfilling life. Then we bombard God to make Him want what we want.

The only things that will really matter at the end are the things that matter to God.

However, at the end of the day and what will be realized at the end of the age is that there is something that God wants. There is something that matters to Him. At the end of the age we can be sure of one thing—God will have exactly what God wants, and what mattered to God all along will absolutely matter to Him at the very end.

I would suggest that the only things that will really matter at the end are the things that matter to God. It is imperative for us to understand what those things are so our hearts and lives can properly be aligned to them; to live a life that matters—not just to the world, meaning worldly significance, but to God. The world and God at times find significance in very different places. If we want to walk worthy of the call, we must know what God wants.[18]

If we want to walk worthy of the call, we must know what God wants.

The enemy was not only after an immediate penalty for Adam and Eve. Don't get me wrong; the enemy definitely understands there are immediate consequences for sin. Sin is devastating. It isn't looking to date you for a season. It is looking to master you.[19] The enemy comes to steal, kill, and destroy.[20]

He is not trying to be your buddy. He creates the perfect trap through the offering of immediate satisfaction and the gratification of lustful desires. He offers you what you think you want, something that will satisfy a craving on the inside of you, and all the while he is masterfully plotting on how this one little seemingly harmless moment of enjoyment can ultimately ruin your life and derail your entire destiny in God.

---

[18] See Eph 4:1
[19] See Gen 4:7
[20] John 10:10

That may sound a little extreme to you, but it is true. It is very true. It is his plan. He wants to ruin your life through sin in an immediate sense, but what he is ultimately after is severing you from God's love and leadership in your life now and then disconnecting you from the ultimate desire God has for those whom He created—which is to be with Him forever as the suitable companion, the bride, for His Son, Jesus, and all of what that implies.

Death was introduced into the human narrative through Adam and Eve's choice to compromise and enter sin. Death was not an initial part of the plan. Adam and Eve were going to reign with God forever, multiplying through being fruitful and having children, and extend the boundaries of the garden to the furthest parts of creation.

Intimate communion with God would be the platform from which they were to extend dominion, subdue the earth, and steward creation. Sin interrupted the plan. Sin brought in death. Sin seemed to be the effective tool to create a wedge between man and the desires God had for man.

The plan God had formed seemed to be derailed because He would have to deal with sin. The enemy knew if he could get sin into man that God would have to change His plan for man because sin could not be factored in as part of that plan. At least this is what the enemy thought.

His self-perceived masterful plan seemed to be succeeding. He figured that he had thought about it from every angle and come up with a strategy that didn't leave room for any loopholes or work-arounds. But in case you are not aware, God is always up to something, and He has a way to make a way when there seems to be no way.[21] He is masterful too.

The enemy never thought God would continue His plans for man by becoming one Himself.

The enemy thought if he could get sin into man that God would have to do away with man. This is what the enemy thought, and in certain ways this would be correct, unless God had other intentions. The enemy never thought God would continue His plans for man by becoming one Himself. The enemy never factored in the possibility of God to do the unthinkable and become a man Himself to provide the solution to the issue and consequences of sin.

God becoming a man would be problematic for the situation the enemy thought he was master-fully crafting. Could God, the holy, eternal, and

---

[21] See Isa 43:16-19

all-powerful, really become a man? Even if He could, would He? We know that answer ended up being yes.

God is holy. He is set apart. There is no one and nothing like Him in the entire universe. Sin complicates things because where God is, sin is not welcome. It's not that it isn't welcome because God doesn't like it and He is too into Himself and His own preferences. Sin is a fundamentally different substance than what God is, and therefore the two cannot coexist in the same space.

When Moses cried out to see the glory of God, God told him that no man could see Him and live.[22] This is the issue. Sin placed a corruption in man, and that corruption cannot reside in the perfection of the presence of God.

God's intentions for man were compromised because man chose to compromise. Compromise brought in corruption. That corruption became an inheritance.[23] That inheritance threw a monkey wrench into the system. Death was now a consequence that had to fall on humanity because man chose to sin.

The enemy understood that God would not compromise His own system and His own standards. The enemy found a way to work from within the boundaries of what God had already set up and

---

[22] Ex 33:20
[23] Rom 5:12

attempted to bring it all down from the inside. Adam and Eve's choice seemed to be just the right in he was looking for.

The enemy finally thought he found a way to manipulate God's righteousness and use it against Him and the things He desired. You can almost hear it this way from the enemy's perspective of it all, "Aha, now I've got You! I know You won't compromise Your own standards or system. I know You are God, but You will never bend the rules even if You could do that to satisfy what it is You want. I've gotten them to sin! You will now have to forfeit Your plans for them. I have found a way to use Your own righteousness and justice against You."

Have you ever considered that God is committed to His own standards? He believes in His judgments and His commandments. He does so because He knows He is right. He knows His way is best. He is not going to change His mind about it. The enemy knows this about God. Therefore the issue of sin was thought to be a power play because the enemy knew God would have to do something to deal with sin.

The wage of sin is death. The enemy thought God would deviate from His original plans, having now been thwarted, because of the now-unavoidable issue of death. No, think again. God is going to put death to rest. His plan was to rest in death and in doing so put death to rest by resurrecting from the dead.

God absolutely believes in His standards. He also believes in the systems He has formed. In fact, He believes in them so much so that He would rather subject Himself to His own standards—unto the laying down of His own life—rather than choose to compromise His own ways. He believes He is right to the point that He chose to yield Himself in humility in becoming a human to His own sense of being right and the penalty associated with His own righteousness and justice.

God chose to come under His own judgments to take upon Himself the full penalty that was required.

God chose to become a sacrifice unto His own system rather than sidestepping the issue or providing a different work-around. God chose to come under His own judgments to take upon Himself the full penalty that was required. Who is this God? Who is this King of Glory?

God wouldn't compromise what He knew was right even when it could benefit His own life and create an easier pathway forward. This must alter the way we think of God. We want to see Him rightly, as He is, and not always as we would prefer Him to be. We mustn't think God will compromise His standards for us to make things easier for us. He won't compromise His ways to make Himself more palatable to us when we want a God that is easier to deal with or more flexible in His judgments.

He would not do this to preserve His own life. Rather, He chose to lay down His own life because He knows He is right and that no other could offer a sacrifice that would satisfy the system He formed. In the bottom of the ninth when humanity was down by a lot and there seemed to be no hope, God subbed Himself into the game. We must allow this to inform our hearts about who He really is.

God is loving. God is just. These two realities are bound in a beautiful tension that can only make real sense in God. He is simultaneously and consistently both. These are not mutually exclusive ideas in God. Because God is just, He had to deal with the issue of sin. Because He is loving, He had to deal with the issue of sin. His banishing was a demonstration of loving justice.

Although God would banish Adam and Eve from the garden, He was already sure of how He would remedy the seemingly impossible situation and reconcile man back to His desires. Death seemed to reign for a time, that is until God entered it and was raised to life on the other side of it, and with Him, our hope. Praise God!

Sin would not rewrite the conclusion of God's story. Sin would not win in redefining the eternal longing that rests in the heart of God. Not at all. It would not have the final say. God is committed to what He wants. God was still working. He was going to reveal exactly how He would continue to provide the way for man to become everything He originally intended. It was going to come at a time and through a way that no one, including the rulers of the age, ever saw coming.

God would do the unfathomable. He would do it to keep in step with His dream and the fulfilling of what it is He is after. Sin would not make man what it wanted and then that be it. No. God would create a pathway for man to be reconciled to what He has always wanted and wanted them to be.

Sin wants to make you into something; it is an issue of becoming. Sin desires for you to become something God never intended for you to be. God has desires for those whom He created, but so does the enemy. There is a battle being waged over the destiny of humanity. Sin was the power play the enemy made in an attempt to put God into a sort of checkmate position. However, God had His own power play. What the enemy did affected everything, that is until God did what He did. God's move was not to "counter"; it was to "conquer."

God has conquered all the enemy's desires and accusations through the life of His Son. And now it is through the life of His Son and the power of the Holy Spirit that He is radically reconfiguring humanity. God's desire is to conform humans to the image of His Son.[24] His desires will be accomplished; He will have what He wants.

God's desire is to conform humans to the image of His Son.

---

[24] Rom 8:29

CHAPTER TWO

IMMEDIATE EVALUATION, ETERNAL IMPLICATIONS

God has a desire. That may sound strange because when you think of God you probably come to certain conclusions. Some of those might be: He is God. He is all-powerful. He doesn't have any needs. All of those are right to think because they are all true.

When thinking that God is all-powerful, we probably also think that cancels out the thought of God having a desire for anything. If God is all-powerful, doesn't that mean that all His needs are taken care of? If God were needy, shouldn't it void the idea of Him being all-powerful? The idea of being all-powerful also assumes that in your power you should be able to produce whatever insufficiency you have.

God is all-powerful. He is also all-sufficient. There is nothing He needs. This may seem fundamental or nonsensical to some, but it is actually very important that we create the proper frame to be able to see Him rightly. But just because He doesn't need anything doesn't mean there aren't things He wants.

There are things He wants. God has a desire. And what He wants creates the motivations for why it is He is doing what He is doing. What is God doing, you ask? God is readying all things for exactly what it is in His heart that He wants. All things are working together for good.

God is a family man. He is after a family.

God is a family man. He is after a family. This family will be a beautiful people. A people from every tribe, every nation, every tongue. A redeemed, born-again, and transformed people that have pledged their allegiance to His Son, Jesus, as the rightful King of the hearts and lives and the creation itself.

This people will be a people that span across every generation from the beginning of time until the final curtain call when Jesus splits the skies and together we all see the Son of Man come riding on the clouds with a host of angels in all the power, authority, and glory of His Father.[25]

This people will be a people that love the Son of Man, Jesus, more than any and every other. It is

---

[25] See Matt 16:27; 1 Thess 4:16-17

with this people that the Father will have the family He desires. This people will be the bride, a suitable companion, for His Son. This people will enjoy Him forever and rule alongside of Him in creation for eternity. This will fulfill the family the Father has always desired.

The fulfillment of this family is very important to the Father. He has gone to great lengths to make sure His desire will be the conclusion all of time and history arrive at. This people are very important to the Son. He has done what no other could do to secure the fulfillment of all His Father desires.

This people are currently being readied by the power of the Holy Spirit. The Holy Spirit is working out what seems like mission impossible—a bride without spot, wrinkle, or blemish, the Father will give as the prize possession of the Son on that great occasion of the marriage supper of the Lamb.[26] The Father, the Son, and the Spirit are all in and together in accomplishing the eternal longing, the dream that has set all things in motion as we know them to be.

It is beautiful and very much needed to understand what it is God wants at the end. Knowing what it is God wants at the end provides for us the necessary information and inspiration to align our lives correctly

---

[26] Eph 5:27; Rev 19:7

in the time we call now. What is ultimate helps to better inform and inspire what is immediate, because there is something very specific God is after at the end and it will come to pass just as He has desired all along.

In fact, there is no plan of the devil that can defeat or derail what God has already set in motion.

There is no plan of the devil that can defeat or derail what God has already set in motion.

We look forward with great anticipation and our hearts burn for what it is God has prepared for those that love Him.[27] But what is amazing is that this isn't some new plan God chose through an audible of sorts, an audible meaning a sudden change of plans as the result of a change in strategy. No, in fact, this has been the plan all along. His plan is the desire that has filled His heart that set all things into motion. All of time and history is serving this purpose, God's eternal purpose.

Time is a tool God Himself has created, and He is using it to serve His purpose. That means that time is not God; God is God. God is not subject to time; He is Lord over time. And because He is Lord over time, He is employing time to serve the purposes He has set into motion. Time is a tool, and it is being used

---

[27] 1 Cor 2:9

to assist in the accomplishment of God having everything He has desired and determined to have. He is God over the whole timeline, and the whole timeline is being superintended by Him.

You could say that all of time serves two ultimate purposes. There are a bunch of other things that are happening in time, sure, and I am sure there are other purposes they are serving. But there are two definite purposes time is serving, and they are ultimate. One would be so that God can reveal Himself in the person of Jesus. The second is so He can ready the people that will love and enjoy His Son forever as they rule all of creation alongside of Him as the companion He deserves.[28]

God doesn't issue promises that He is not confident and certain He can make good on.

These are two purposes to which all other purposes are serving or being served by. It is amazing. God's wisdom to orchestrate all things unto and into what He wants is matchless. He is all-powerful, so He can perform that which He promises. He doesn't issue promises that He is not confident and certain He can make good on.

---

[28] Samuel Whitefield. *Discipleship Begins with Beholding* (Grandview, MO: One King Publishing, 2020), 8.

You can look at the very beginning of creation and find God's desires present. From the beginning of the Bible, in the opening book, Genesis, we see a clear picture of what was in God's heart all along. After

This is always the promise: whatever God forms He promises to fill.

God forms all things, He fills all things. This is always the promise: whatever God forms He promises to fill. He makes man last. Forms him from the dust of the earth. His crowning achievement. He gets face-to-face with him and breathes life into him and then Adam becomes a living being.[29]

After Adam comes alive to God, God places him in the Garden of Eden. It is here that Adam will learn how to intimately relate to God and be a good steward of all God has entrusted to him. Adam will learn intimacy and responsibility because God has a desire to share with Adam His authority.

After creating Adam, we don't make it too far into the story before we get an incredible piece of evidence. Right after the description of the garden in Genesis chapter 2 and the command from God about His regulations with the trees, a peculiar verse immediately follows. The Bible tells us that God is investigating

[29] Gen 2:7, NASB

the situation with Adam. God is surveying the situation and comes to a conclusion I would love for us to consider afresh. Sometimes it is the things we think we already know that stunt us from knowing the things God longs to reveal to us. So let us look again at what is an incredibly familiar passage.

As God is evaluating the situation He has created and how it has progressed, the Bible tells us that He makes this statement, "It is not good for the man to be alone; I will make him a helper suitable for him."[30] Depending on the translation or the version you read, there are several interchangeable words for "suitable." Other translations say: comparable, corresponding, who is just right.[31] Depending on your translation the word helper can be also noted as: companion.[32] So the overall idea generated from this statement is that the Father has a desire to make a companion for the man that will be a suitable and comparable helper. This statement has such profound implications.

We must know that God didn't make a mistake. His wisdom is perfect. He knows what He is doing and how He is doing it. He didn't forget something along the way. He didn't make Adam and then later realize he was dealing with loneliness and He needed

---

[30] Gen 2:18, NASB
[31] ESV; NKJV; NLT
[32] CSB

to solve the dilemma Adam was going through. God is a master builder. So if this isn't what happened, then what is going on? Great question.

With this statement the Bible provides for us we get a clear glimpse into the heart of God's desires. We get to see the end from the beginning. This one statement has enormous value. We need to reapproach this statement and see its consequences. "It is not good for the man to be alone, so I will make a suitable helper for him."

This is an immediate evaluation that also provides eternal implications.

When you see this, you need to understand that this is an immediate evaluation that also provides eternal implications. When you see and read this statement you should also understand it in the context of, "It is not good for the Son of Man to be alone, so I will make ready a suitable and comparable companion for Him." Oh boy, this is where things get amazing!

The Bible is very detailed and is great with communicating certain details because God's desires can be seen in the details. After that statement we find out that God brings all the other animals that had been made before Adam. They go through the adventure of inventorying them and creating names for them. Awesome.

Then at the end of this process we learn that among them all there would be none of them that were a helper suitable for Adam.[33] So with none to be found that matched the criteria of what God desired, we find God working on behalf of what is in His heart.

God causes a deep sleep to fall upon Adam. After Adam is laid down in this deep sleep God performs a surgery of sorts. He opens Adam's side. He takes out a rib. With the rib He takes out of the pierced side of Adam He forms the companion He desires for him. God fashions woman from the rib and then brings the woman to Adam.

Adam is awakened. Upon being awakened, the Father presents to Adam the companion His desire produced for him. Adam clings to his new helper and companion and the two enter a covenant relationship. They will together steward God's desires for creation. This is beautiful in every way. But we know we can see the end from the beginning. Can you see it?

Jesus is referenced as the last Adam.[34] Here the reference for Adam is a reference to a version of humanity. Adam was the first version of human and represented all of humanity. That is why when he sinned it fell on all of humanity as an inheritance.[35]

---

[33] Gen 2:19-20
[34] 1 Cor 15:45, NASB
[35] Rom 5:12

Jesus is referenced as the last Adam because He is the perfect version of humanity. There never needs to be another, so He is last. It is the final version; He is perfect. Jesus is the prototype. He is the pattern. It is into His image that the Father has predestined all others that come to love Him to be conformed into.[36]

With Jesus referenced as the last Adam, it is wild to see how the last Adam and the first Adam entered a similar process that would produce the desires the Father has for them. Adam gives us a glimpse of Jesus. Jesus is the fulfillment of Adam. Adam is the original man. Jesus is the Son of Man. It is not good for the man to be alone. It is not good for the Son of Man to be alone. Let's look at some of the similarities.

Adam was laid into a deep sleep. Jesus was laid down into a deep sleep. We know Jesus was laid into much more than a deep sleep. Jesus was crucified and died. They laid Him in a grave. He went beneath the earth and into hell itself.[37] Adam's side was pierced and a rib was taken out which would provide the means as to how the Father would form the companion He desired for him.

Jesus' side was pierced. His skin and the veil were torn. Blood and water poured forth from Him.[38] The

---

[36] Rom 8:29
[37] John 19:41
[38] John 19:34

Father uses the blood and the water to form and ready the companion He desires for His Son.[39]

Adam was awakened from his deep sleep. Jesus was raised from the dead. He was resurrected by the power of the Holy Spirit. He is alive, the firstborn from the dead, an eternal and glorified human.[40] The Father presented the companion He made for Adam to the man. His bride was ready. Adam was able to enter a covenant relationship with his bride and cling to her. This is where the story takes a little shift.

Jesus thinks His bride is to die for.

Adam immediately fully realized his relationship with the bride the Father formed for him. Jesus isn't yet able to do that the way He fully desires to. Have you considered that Jesus laid down His life to fully secure everything His Father desires? Part of what His Father desires is this bride He will one day present to His Son. The presentation day has not happened yet. Adam had his presentation day, but Jesus has not. We are all headed toward the marriage supper of the Lamb.[41]

Jesus is still waiting for His bride. This is no small thing. Jesus thinks His bride is to die for. He longs for

---

[39] Rom 6:4; Eph 5:26
[40] Rom 1:4; Acts 10:40; Col 1:18; 1 Pet 1:3
[41] Rev 19:7

that great day of presentation. He has done His part to make sure the people He deserves can be fully His, the way He and His Father have always desired. Adam got his bride; the Father is still readying one for Jesus.

Adam got his bride; the Father is still readying one for Jesus.

Adam was able to cling to the companion the Father formed for him. Jesus has given His life as a pledge of devotion to the forming of this people, and His heart is burning in intercession as they are being readied for His day of clinging He knows is coming.[42]

When Jesus said, "It is finished,"[43] on that day from the cross He wasn't simply talking about His own immediate life. It was this and more He was speaking of. Jesus was saying He had finished the job. All the work that needed to be done for His Father to have everything He wanted had been completed. He had done what no other could do. He finished it. Everything His Father had ever dreamed of, prophesied, and promised, could now be fully realized. He had made a way where there seemed to be no way. Jesus has overcome.

Jesus has done His part, which is the most important part. However, all the work isn't finished.

---

[42] Heb 7:25
[43] John 19:30

28

There is obviously still much to do. The bride, the helper and companion He deserves, must be formed; the bride must be readied. Now that Jesus' part has been accomplished it is the power of His own Spirit, the Holy Spirit, that is readying for Him the bride He desires and deserves.

Jesus has offered up His own life. The Spirit has been poured out. The task will be accomplished. This isn't an *if*, it is a *when*. Jesus will have what His Father promised because His Father doesn't make a promise unless He knows He is able to make good on it.

The bride is made up of the people that have abandoned all other lovers and put their hope and trust in Jesus as their Savior and Lord.

The bride is made up of the people that have abandoned all other lovers and put their hope and trust in Jesus as their Savior and Lord. They are born again. They bear His Spirit. They are being conformed to His image. They walk in His power. They love Him above all things.

They love what He loves and hate what He hates. They have found life in Him and are joyfully willing to lose their lives for Him. Yes, this is His bride! They are wild and they are free. They are powerful.

This bride is made up of a new creation. They are new creatures. They are a new version of humanity.

They are products of God's desire and power. The bride must be made up of a new creation. In fact, it is another one of the ways God has chosen to both reveal Himself and glorify Himself—through this people that have been radically transformed by being conformed to the image of His Son.

It is this people that will be comparable to Jesus by being conformed to His image that will be the suitable bride He deserves. Yes, the bride, this powerful new version of humanity is a necessity! In the next chapter we will discuss further the need for a new creation.

CHAPTER THREE

THE NEED FOR A NEW CREATION

The Bible creates two categories of people. It is right for the Bible to do this because there are not more than two. I know that may be startling to consider because you can probably think of dozens of categories the world has created to know how to suitably label people to properly interact with people.

This is what the world may do, but this is not what the Bible does. The Bible reduces things down to a very simple place and starts there. All these other ways to identify people come after these first two foundational categories.

Things get simple when we allow the Bible to say what it is saying instead of making it say what we want it to say, what we think would be easier for us to deal with. We should come to the Bible as the authoritative Word of God, the source of absolute truth. From there, we then take that truth and let it bring transformation to our hearts and the way we think. This is the way it is supposed to be.

Some try to get God to think more like them. To do that they must massage and manipulate the Scriptures in an attempt to endorse their own thoughts and desires for their own sense of truth. This is not what God is doing. He is not thinking more like us. He wants us to think more like Him.

We should come to the Bible as the authoritative Word of God, the source of absolute truth.

This requires us coming to the Word as the ultimate source of truth and the governing authority in and over our lives and allowing those words to change the way we think and live. And with that there are two categories of people the Bible mentions: those who are dead in their trespasses; and those who have been made alive to God.[44]

These two categories include all people. There is no other category for this specific conversation the Bible takes note of. I know the line here seems to be a little drastic. I know there are probably immediate feelings towards what is being communicated, but we

---

[44] Eph 2:1

must let the Bible say what it is saying and then allow God to conform our lives to that.

These categories are clear. There are only two options for existence and the way one's life can be lived out. You are either dead in your trespasses, or you have become alive to God. That's it. Those are the two categories.

Jesus stated it just as clearly in His conversation with Nicodemus in the third chapter of John's gospel. Jesus said Himself, "Truly, truly, I say to you, unless one is born again, he cannot see the kingdom of God. . . . Truly, truly, I say to you, unless one is born of water and the Spirit, he cannot enter the kingdom of God. That which is born

> **We must let the Bible say what it is saying and then allow God to conform our lives to that.**

of the flesh is flesh, and that which is born of the Spirit is spirit. Do not be amazed that I say to you, 'You must be born again.' "[45]

Being born again is necessary. The only way to come out of your sins and your trespasses is to be born again. The world fell under a particular bondage because of the effects of the garden and the inheritance of sin and death. There is a tyranny to corruption that

---

[45] John 3:3-7, NASB

all of creation is experiencing. Man has fallen victim and subject to powers and principalities.

The influence of the enemy, also known as the sway of the wicked one, has a certain jurisdiction that right now is in effect until the return of King Jesus. He will dethrone every ruler and power and establish His unending Kingdom in a very real geopolitical way.[46] His reign will be forever. Our hearts burn for that day.

The only way to come out of your sins and your trespasses is to be born again.

John says that right now the whole world is under the sway of the wicked one.[47] Sway can be defined in a few ways, and it is important to bring better definition to what John is communicating so we can better get our bearings for what he is saying.

One of the ways sway can be defined is: to move or incline to one side or in a particular direction. Another definition is: to cause (the mind, emotions, etc., or a person) to incline or turn in a specified way; influence. And lastly, one more way to define it is: to dominate; direct, to wield as a weapon or scepter, to rule; govern.

The sway of the wicked one is not to be taken lightly. The whole world is under its influence. The

---

[46] See Dan 7:9-14
[47] 1 John 5:19

idea being communicated here is that there is a particular direction the enemy is moving the entire world by the wielding of his influence. Powers and principalities have desires. These desires are being wielded throughout the world.

These powers and principalities, also known as the rulers of the age, are using their influence as a weapon to derail people from God's desires and to bring an eternal disruption to the purpose God has for them. This may sound simple, but it is not to be taken lightly, for it is no small matter at all.

The opening of Ephesians chapter 2 creates more definition to the point we are making here. Paul, after saying that you were dead in your trespasses and sins, gives the idea of what the prince of the power of the air is looking to accomplish and how it affects our lives. Paul says the reason you were dead in your trespasses and sins is because, "You formerly walked according to the course of this world, according to the prince of the power of the air, of the spirit that is now at work in the sons of disobedience. Among them we too all formerly lived in the lusts of our flesh, indulging in the desires of the flesh and mind, and were by nature children of wrath, even as the rest."[48]

---

[48] Eph 2:2-4, NASB1995

Here we have the condition of the world and its categories. Paul lays them out clearly, and just like John and Jesus communicated, there seems to only be two. To John, you are either under the sway of the wicked one, or you are not. To Paul, you are either walking according to the course of this world, living under the prince of the power of the air, operating in and bound by a spirit of disobedience, or you are not. The options are few and they are clear.

It is important to take note of what exactly the powers of the air are looking to accomplish when you are living according to the course of the world. We already read over it, but let's look one more time because there is a tendency to overlook the objective of powers and principalities and therefore miss one of the primary ways their influence is wielded into and against our hearts.

Paul says we too all formerly lived in the lusts of our flesh, indulging in the desires of the flesh and the mind. This means the influence being wielded against us wants us to live from a place where we indulge in whatever we want (the flesh) or whatever we think (the mind) is best.

I know you might think this is harmless initially. However, when you live this out a little, you very quickly realize that what we feel we want and/or what we think is best, is not always what is best for us and/

or everybody else around us. This gets very bad very fast. You do not have to search very far to see how this type of paradigm for life is destructive.

We do not have the capacity to determine what is best. I don't want that to be offensive; it is not intended that way at all. We are not God; He alone is God. God alone has the capacity to determine what is best. Those determiners and boundaries

What we feel we want and/or what we think is best, is not always what is best for us.

help govern the creation He made. We are limited. We are finite. We are the creatures and not the God who made the creatures.

We did not make the environment the creatures would live in. We are those who have been made, fearfully and wonderfully made, as David would say.[49] Therefore, we are limited in our makeup because we have been made and are not the Maker. Even though this is very true, we at times still want to think we know better than we do.

One of the consequences of the garden is that man now thinks he knows what's best. If you remember what happened when Adam and Eve were going to eat of the tree, the enemy told them something very

---

[49] Ps 139:14

specific. While the interaction was happening between the serpent and Eve, he told her, "You surely will not die! For God knows that in the day you eat from it (the tree) your eyes will be opened, and you will be like God, knowing good and evil."[50]

The idea here is not just the acknowledgement of good and evil. The idea here is that Adam and Eve would become enlightened. Their eyes would be opened and they would be able to make determinations, like God, on what was good and what was evil. They would have the ability to bring evaluation to issues of morality. This sounds inviting, but it was incredibly manipulative and became devastating. We are still dealing with its effects today.

Adam and Eve ate of the tree. Their eyes were opened. Yes, they realized their nakedness. But now they would also have to deal with the effects of having their eyes opened. Seeming to now be enlightened, they would have the power to reason for themselves on what was best for them.

This enlightening has fallen upon all of humanity. At the end of the day, we want to be able to do what we want, how we want. Without realizing it, what we are really saying is that the lustful desires of our hearts

---

[50] Gen 3:4-5, NASB1995

and minds should be what is allowed to govern the life we have decided we want to live.

Ultimately, and you might not say it this way, but it is the condition of the situation and something that must be acknowledged—we want to be God over our own life. We want to be God over our own life because it is offensive to think that there is someone more powerful than we are who knows better than we do what is best for us. The only issue here is that we do not make a good God for our life.

God is a very good God; He is great as a matter of fact. He knows He is a great God. He knows He is the Supreme Being, better than any other, and He is very capable and very good at being God. He also knows that you and I are not very capable, and not very good at being our own God. He has filled the role. It requires our acknowledgment and our repentance from all our own attempts to have things our way.

The enemy is a master manipulator. His attempt to sway the world is not always something that is noticed. It seems to fly under the radar in most instances. In the beginning it always seems harmless, and why? Most times because it offers you something you think will satisfy a desire you have.

The enemy wields influence against you by offering you something you may want or think is best. The invitation is sown in your heart or mind. Then it is engaged and acted upon. Once acted upon you demonstrate, live out, or manifest that desire.

One of the ways the enemy's desires get manifested throughout the world is through the feelings and thoughts he wields into and against the hearts of people. These thoughts create a sway in humanity and create the course of the world. The enemy moves people from God's desires and His loving leadership, many times through the indulging of the feelings of the heart and the thoughts of the mind. We do what we want and move away from what God wants.

There are times when we think we are doing what we want, and we are really doing what the enemy wants.

There are times when we think we are doing what we want, and we are really doing what the enemy wants. But that is the issue. We feel like we are doing what we want. However, the thoughts or feelings as to what we should want have been introduced to us via the influence of powers and principalities. So are you doing what you want? Maybe. But is it really what you want if enemy forces have provided you with what you think you should want? Here is the sway.

It happens so fast. From one moment to the next you find yourself engaged in warfare by way of the influence from the powers of the air that are infiltrating your life. The battle has ensued. The potential carnage is real. Chaos is creating an inner swirl. And most of the time we are unaware of what is happening when it is happening.

We are unaware because we are not discerning according to the terms Paul has laid out in Ephesians. We are trained and constantly conditioned by our culture to believe that whatever we want is what we should be able to have. Whatever I want to do is what I should be able to do.

All of life attempts to reduce things down to the pursuit of my own independent satisfaction.

All of life, according to the system of the age and the sway of the wicked one, attempts to reduce things down to the pursuit of my own independent satisfaction—where I ultimately get to determine what will satisfy me, and then pursue and participate in those items without concern of some overarching authority constantly reminding me that I should not be able to do so.

We want to do things our own way and live out our own truth. Truth gets discounted and diminished to something that is relative rather than absolute. Relative to my own feelings and thoughts, and therefore more personal in nature and constantly conditional, rather than something that is corporate and absolute—a one size fits all.

Who says I can't marry whomever I want? Who says I can't be physically attracted to whomever I want? Who's to say I can't be sexually attracted to whomever it is I want? Who's to say I am not supposed to be sexually involved with whomever it is I think I want to be? Who's to say I can't do whatever I want with the baby forming inside my body? After all, it is my body, right? I should be able to do whatever I feel is best with my own body, right?

Who says I can't think I am biologically a boy if I was born a girl? Who says it's wrong if you kill someone? Who says it's wrong if you cheat on your spouse? Who's to say it isn't right if I want to choose whatever I think is the best of all available options? Do you see what is happening? These are just a handful of examples.

Once this box is opened, the downward spiral happens incredibly quickly. But who says that none of these things are right? If I feel they are right, isn't that all that matters? If I think it is best, isn't that all that matters? No, that is not all that matters. What matters most is what God says. He is God; we are not.

He has created boundaries for creation through His own loving intentions and wisdom that hold all things together. What He says is right. What He says is best. What He says should govern our lives, but because of the sway of the wicked one and the course of the world, it doesn't always happen that way.

The tyranny of the powers of the air is real. John and Paul spoke about these two categories so we would be able to see and think clearly. Why does the drawing of lines have to be so clear? Because the world does a great job of creating other categories. The world would tell you there are more categories than just the two we are describing here.

The world would say you can be a good person. It would identify and acknowledge that there are people who do bad things. There are even wicked people who create a life set on intentionally doing things evil and vile in nature. But you don't have to be like those people; you can be a good person.

A good person is someone who isn't a murderer, a thief or criminal, an adulterer, someone who doesn't beat their kids or physically and/or verbally abuse their spouse. A good person is someone who isn't like these bad people we have mentioned that the world identifies are real and bad.

A good person is morally and ethically good for the most part. Everybody has their mistakes. Everybody deserves a little grace. Everybody can have a bad day. But a bad day doesn't make you an overall bad person, does it?

The world and your own conscience will tell you there is another category. This other category is for people that are good people. They aren't serving the devil. They aren't bound by the powers of the air. But they also haven't been, like Jesus said to Nicodemus, born again. They aren't alive to God. But they aren't also alive to the influence of the enemy. They are the people we think exist in this "other" category.

People are either bound to their sin and dead in their trespasses, or they have been born again and are alive to God and in relationship with His Son by the power of His Spirit.

They are nice people. They have good hearts. They do good things. They are involved in their community. They give to charity. They don't do anything observable that is classified as wrong or bad. These people are good. These are the people for whom we try to make things seem better for them than they are.

Here is the thing; you may give these people you have determined are good people grace because you understand the consequences for people under the sway of the wicked one and live according to the course of the world, but do the Scriptures? Does God graciously create the extra category the same way you do?

With all your best efforts to create more categories for people, at the end of the day, and more importantly, at the end of the age, there will remain only two. People are either bound to their sin and dead in their trespasses, living under the tyranny of corruption to the powers of the air and according to the current course of this world, or they have been born again and are alive to God and in relationship with His Son by the power of His Spirit. Those are the only options. Being born again and becoming a new creation are the only ways out of the category you may be living in, which is dead in sin and your trespasses.

This is where the issue of our response to the Gospel is not some side issue or peripheral matter. That is because the issue of the Gospel is not an issue of bad people or good people. This issue is that there are two categories of people: those who are dead, and those who are alive. Those who are born again, and those who are not. According to the Scripture and to God, there are none that are good and that are doing good that are not born again.

We tend to evaluate things by what is observable of someone's life. What we can see. The things we can visibly have evidence of. Whatever we witness or don't witness a lot of times is how we build our cases as to how someone may be doing. The problem with this is that our observance or lack thereof of corruption that is external and visible in nature is not all that matters. It may be what matters to us, but it is not all that matters.

God sees what you and I do not see. God's evaluation is very different than ours. This is what matters. God takes notice of an internal corruption. A corruption that is many times not visible to the natural eye. A cancer that often is eating away at the condition of our soul. A sickness that cannot be remedied by behavioral modification techniques.

Being born again brings you out of the category of death and radically translates you into the category of life.

This condition can only be healed through the power that God supplies to those who respond rightly to the Gospel by repenting, pledging their allegiance to His Son, receiving the indwelling power and life of the Holy Spirit, and experience being born again. Being born again brings you out of the category of death and radically translates you into the category of life.

Paul emphasized to the believers in Rome a need to be transformed. He exhorted them to "not be conformed to this world, but be transformed by the renewing of your mind, so that you may prove what the will of God is, that which is good and acceptable and perfect."[51]

Transformation and not just behavior modification is needed. You cannot just paint the outside of the building when everything on the inside is rotting. Jesus rebuked Pharisees for this. He called them hypocrites. He called them whitewashed tombs, beautiful on the outside but bankrupt on the inside.[52]

Man has become masterful at creating the right religious filter for his life. There has always been an attempt to hide the internal corruption by way of putting up the right exterior. Saying right and doing right does not always mean that what is going on from the inside is right. Sin has created an internal issue that must be dealt with. The flood of corruption on the inside is in desperate need of a deliverer.

Just as Noah built a giant boat that would bring deliverance to his generation from the flood of his day, God has put together His own beautiful plan to bring deliverance and salvation to all of humanity through a

> **Transformation and not just behavior modification is needed. You cannot just paint the outside of the building when everything on the inside is rotting.**

---

[51] Rom 12:2, NASB
[52] Matt 23:27-28

man that He would send. This deliverer has not only come to deliver from the tidal wave of corruption on the outside, but He has come to set us free from the f lood of corruption and the bondage of the sway on the inside. Praise God!

The way you behave is in accordance with the nature that you have; that is why it comes so natural to you.

The accusation of the enemy, the tyranny of sin, and the demand of the grave will never be satisfied through the right religious behaviors. Behavioral modification tells you that you can just try harder, be more disciplined. This may be accurate for trying to change what is happening on the outside. But this issue is not what is happening on the outside.

The issue is that there is something happening on the inside that you do not have the power to change. You cannot change it because it is what we consider to be natural. We were born this way. It is natural because it is our nature. The way you behave is in accordance with the nature that you have; that is why it comes so natural to you.

You need a different nature. You need to be reconfigured at a default level. But how? Great question. And once again, God has a plan. God's plan was not to change His mind and do away with man altogether.

When things seemed to be completely hopeless, God did the unthinkable, the unimaginable.

At the darkest hour, God let the Son rise. God became a man. God put Himself into man so that His Spirit could have access to man internally to produce the powerful change of nature that was needed.

Throughout history God's Spirit had rested on men externally, and that was fitting for that time, but God's goal was to completely invade and possess the lives of men internally. God knew that to change men from the inside He would need to get on the inside. He had a plan. He had already committed Himself to the way.

God's plan to change the condition man had fallen into would be to become a man Himself. The Godman would create the proper path for man to come back to God! The great reconciliation endeavor was in the works. God would work Himself into man to work out His desires for man. It would be extraordinary. In our next chapter we will investigate the man, Jesus, that has broken open the pathway and provided the power for our passover!

At the darkest hour, God let the Son rise. God became a man.

CHAPTER FOUR

THE PROVISION AND POWER FOR EXODUS

The actual substance of what is inside of man must be changed. The external imagery of success will not be able to hide away forever the inevitable exposure of the internal bankruptcy that is, like a cancer, devouring the insides of man. Man can seem to keep it all together on the outside, but God knows very well what is happening on the inside.

The issue of sin, for as well as man thinks he can behave,

The ultimate issue is not behaving; it is becoming.

will always keep him in a place where he can be seen "doing right" and still not necessarily "be right." All of this is because there is an issue. The issue is not just with how developed or underdeveloped we may be perceived to be in our ability to create and keep the image alive. It is not a matter of how long we can sustain a well-behaved life. That is because the ultimate issue is not behaving; it is becoming. Man must become something different than what he inherited when he was born.

Man is not right. Not right according to the ultimate desire that God has for man. Sin is still creating the chasm from the original intentions God has for His people. Therefore, sin must have a resolve. There must be a solution provided for the issue of sin if man is to be reconciled to God and His loving intentions that moved Him to create. The

There must be a solution provided for the issue of sin if man is to be reconciled to God and His loving intentions that moved Him to create.

eternal consequence that sin has created must find a remedy. If sin is not dealt with, then there cannot be a forever with God after death. This is a big deal.

Sin creates complications. We don't understand how big of a deal the issue of sin and the sin nature are because it is a situation we have been born into. All our life has been spent dealing with and experiencing the effects of sin. Sin has saturated everything.

It is somewhat unfathomable for us to consider that there will come a day when Jesus returns and He will deal with the issue of sin forever, in an eternal way. He will completely rid creation of the ongoing effects of sin, and all will be perfectly reconciled into and unto an obedience to the loving righteousness of His Father.

Sin is the inherent corruption within us that desires to rebel against God and His loving leadership for our lives. Sin is the substance and the power at work that longs to create independence from God. It wants its own way. It makes us rebels. It creates hostility towards God.

It is very real, and it is very much a problem. Sin doesn't just want you to have a few moments of enjoyment here and there; it wants to rule over your life and govern it according to its desires.

Sin wants to master you by making you feel like you are capable of being the master of your own life. In doing so,

If sin is not dealt with, then there cannot be a forever with God after death.

you cast off God's leadership and loving boundaries, supposing to rule over your own life, and eventually end up becoming mastered by what made you feel like you were capable of being the master. Sin doesn't just want to entice; it wants to govern. It doesn't just promise momentary satisfaction without the intended hook of subjection.

Sin has desires. The Bible tells us that when lust has conceived, it gives birth to sin; and sin, when it has run its course, brings forth death.[53] The ultimate desire of sin is death. Sin wants death. That death is an eternal fate. Sin longs to produce an eternal separation from God. Sin doesn't just want to satisfy you; it wants to separate you. Sin is a wedge, and that wedge has created the need for a solu-tion. Sin cannot be left alone; it must be dealt with.

Sin doesn't just want to satisfy you; it wants to separate you.

Sin is what is natural to man. We have been born into it and all the world and its ways that surround us have been saturated by it. It is what we would call natural, or normal. God would have to create a new normal to deal with the issue of sin and create an open pathway for man to be connected to the purpose He has always desired for him.

A new normal? Yes, a new normal. There would have to be a way for man to experience a new nature, one without the ongoing effects of sin and the corrupt tendencies. But how?

God became a man. This statement, though short, has extended the life and purpose of humanity. God has done what no other could do. He has become as one of us to do what none of us could accomplish. For unto us a child has been born, a son has been given![54]

---

[53] James 1:15, NASB
[54] Isa 9:6

Jesus has really done it. He has overcome. He has lived the perfect life. Though tempted in every way He was without sin.[55] Born of a virgin.[56] Spotless and without blemish. He chose to joyfully embrace the cross and lay down His life.[57] He was executed as one of us. He was raised on behalf of us. Jesus would go into the grave, but He would not remain there. The Father has raised Him from the dead by the power of the Holy Spirit. Jesus is alive!

Jesus is the firstfruit, the first born from the dead. He has been raised, and with Him all the hope for humanity that had been lost. Jesus is a man that is alive on the other side of death. He is resurrected and glorified. He is an eternal human. Upon His ascension, there is now a man in the heavens, seated at the right hand of the Father, and He still bears the scars of His love for His bride. These scars, the rings in His hands, He bears as the eternal symbol of clinging to the bride that He deserves.

> **He has been raised, and with Him all the hope for humanity that had been lost. Jesus is a man that is alive on the other side of death.**

---

[55] Heb 4:15
[56] See Matt 1; Luke 1
[57] Heb 12:2

Jesus lived fully man and fully God. He was a man that was full of the Holy Spirit without measure. It pleased God to put the fullness of who He is into Christ.[58] While He had His time upon the earth with His disciples, He told them it would be better for Him to go because He would send another to be with them.[59]

Jesus was speaking about the Holy Spirit. Jesus knew that what man needed was power. He knew that man needed real power that would produce the needed change on the inside and bring real transformation to his nature and not just his behavior.

If you change your nature your behavior will follow. But if you change your behavior, it will not always guarantee a change in your nature. God is looking to radically transform the substance of what is on the inside, and not just redecorate what is on the outside.

After Jesus was raised from the dead, He told His disciples He was going to send them power from on high so they could be what He desired for them to be and live the life He desired them to live.[60] This power is the promise of the Holy Spirit. The Holy Spirit will come on to man and into man and give man what man needs to be what God desires for him.

---

[58] Col 1:19
[59] John 16:7
[60] Acts 1:8

The magnitude of what God has done and how it affects our lives cannot be overly stated or overexaggerated. God has provided the means necessary for the transformation that so desperately needed to happen in and to man. He has done so through the provision of His own Son, Jesus.

Jesus has become the provision and the power for our exodus.

Jesus has become the provision and the power for our exodus. Because of what Jesus has done we do not have to be who or what we have always been. We can now put our faith and our hope in Jesus as Savior and Lord and be born again. We can yield our heart and life to Jesus and be beautifully filled with the life of His Holy Spirit. In this born-again experience we are what the Bible calls "saved." Saved from what? Saved from the damaging consequences of sin and the death it desires.

Those who are born again are a new creation. Paul says that if any man is in Christ, that man is now a new creature; old things have passed and all things have now become new.[61] He is something entirely different than what he used to be. Though the outside may still be intact and look the same, there is something powerful and radical that has happened and is

---

[61] 2 Cor 5:17

happening in an ongoing way on the inside—a meta-morphosis of sorts!

Old things have passed. The old man has been conquered. The sin nature that was known as normal and had become normalized throughout the experience of life has been put to death. It no longer has dominion. The hostile rebel that used to be very much alive and demanded to have its way continually has been put into the grave. And like Jesus, there is a new man that has been raised up. Through the born-again experience, you can become alive to God and no longer be a slave to sin. You can now be a slave to God and to His righteousness.[62]

Paul had powerful words to speak about this in his letter to the born-again believers in Rome. For the sake of how incredible this is we will not shorten it at all. "For if we have been united with Him like this in His death, we will certainly also be united with Him in His resurrection. We know that our old self was crucified with Him so that the body of sin might be rendered powerless, that we should no longer be slaves to sin. For anyone who has died has been freed from sin. Now if we died with Christ, we believe that we will also live with Him. For we know that since Christ was raised from the dead, He cannot die again; death

---

[62] Rom 6:18

no longer has dominion over Him. The death He died, He died to sin once for all; but the life He lives, He lives to God. So you too must count yourselves dead to sin, but alive to God in Christ Jesus. Therefore do not let sin reign in your mortal body so that you obey its desires. Do not present the parts of your body to sin as instruments of wickedness, but present yourselves to God as those who have been brought

God has provided real grace through the Holy Spirit to produce powerful change in your life.

from death to life; and present the parts of your body to Him as instruments of righteousness. For sin shall not be your master, because you are not under law, but under grace."[63]

God has provided real grace through the Holy Spirit to produce powerful change in your life. This grace is real and the effects of it are extraordinary. Paul recognized the work of this grace in his own heart and life. In fact, Paul knew so well that what had happened in his life could only have been accomplished because of what God had done and now made available that he told the Corinthians, "I am what I am by the grace of God."[64]

---

[63] Rom 6:5-14, BSB
[64] 1 Cor 15:10

Paul knew what he used to be. Religious zealot. Murderer. A broken, corrupt, and sinful man. However, he also knew that what he used to be he was not anymore. Paul was something different than what he used to be, and it was very noticeable to him. It was very noticeable to others. He was not the same man.

We settle for some polish to the old man when God wants to do away with the old man altogether.

Paul saw Jesus. He had an encounter with Jesus that radically changed his life. He became born again. This born-again experience fully dealt with the issue of the old man and provided him the power to become something he never would have been able to accomplish on his own. He was different. It was real. God had done it.

"I am what I am" is the recognition that you are something. It is the awareness that what you are now is not at all what you used to be. This is the issue. Too many times we settle for being a little bit better. We settle for some polish to the old man when God wants to do away with the old man altogether.

We try to be a little bit better version of who we used to be. We are okay to remain with the old cycles, old struggles, and old appetites. We realize that the strength of the old man is still alive and wrestling on the inside of us, yet we attempt to cover him well with religious exteriors.

We are not supposed to settle for a religious version of the old man. God is not looking for religious performers who have perfected the art of covering up their brokenness and corruption. God is not in the cover-up game. This is not God's goal. God's goal is for you to become something entirely different than what you used to be, like Paul, a new creature.

God is not covering the dominance of the self-life; He is conquering the reality of the self-life through the issuing of His own divine life that can now abide within the human life. Divine life conquers the self-life. It is God's way. You need God to be set free from you. You may have power to cover it, but only God can give you power to conquer it.

> **You need God to be set free from you. You may have power to cover it, but only God can give you power to conquer it.**

By the grace of God, Paul recognized the power source of his own transformation. He knew it wasn't simply discipline alone. He acknowledged it wasn't the work of some crafty wisdom that had come through close friends of his. It wasn't just the activities he was participating in that had done it. God had done it.

God had provided the means necessary for this wild and radical work to happen on the inside of him.

There could have been no other way. Paul knew the corruption and how intense it was and that it would take something much more intense than the power of sin and corruption to change it. Thank God He has power to overcome the sin nature that resides on the inside. This power God had imparted to Paul, through His own Spirit, Paul called grace.

Grace is the supernatural power that God imparts to us by His Spirit for us to fulfill His purpose.

The operation of God's grace that Paul knew was working on the inside of him is what he attributed his change to. Grace is the supernatural power that God imparts to us by His Spirit for us to fulfill His purpose. One of those purposes is to look more like His Son, to be conformed to the image of Jesus. Grace works in us to make us more like Jesus. Grace gives us power, and that power is from God and is very real, to be conformed to the image of Jesus.

Grace has an agenda. There is a motive with which grace comes into our lives. Grace is not issued for self-pleasure. Grace is not imparted to satisfy self-indulgence. Grace is missional, and God has already predetermined that mission. Paul had an understanding that grace was given and that grace was up to something in his life.

Like Paul, your becoming is found in beholding. You must look to Jesus. There is no other way. This is the pathway God has laid down. Jesus alone is the way, the truth, and the life. He is real life. He is eternal life. And when you look to Him, He gives life to those who look to

Your becoming is found in beholding. You must look to Jesus.

Him and are in Him to become a new creation, a new creature, a brand-new version of human.

If you are born again, you are a wildly different version of human. You are not the same as everyone else around you. God has put His Spirit in you. God has conquered the sin nature in you. All your old tendencies and appetites have been satisfied through the life of His Son, Jesus, and the work of His Spirit is now powerfully transforming you and conforming you to His image. This is a real work that God has done. You are not the same version of human that you were—you are now a new creature.

If you are born again God wants you to have a restful confidence that He has done a real work on the inside of you. Too many people walk around in guilt, shame, and condemnation. They struggle to believe that God has changed them. They don't live with joy in the beauty of believing the new person that God has made them. They relate more to the old man, all the cycles of sin and struggle they have become so familiar with over time, than they do the redeemed and trans

You must be more impressed with God than you are with sin.

formed version of themselves, which is the work that God has done.

When it all boils down, they don't really believe

they have been born again. There is no real confidence to say, like Paul, "I am what I am by the grace of God." Or they believe they are born again and for whatever reason have a weird belief that sin is more powerful than God and His grace. Let's say this—it is not!

You must be more impressed with God than you are with sin. Sin is not more powerful than God. If you believe and have been born again you have power through the indwelling life of God by His Holy Spirit to deal the eviction notice to the appetite for sin in your life. God's grace is sufficient.

There must come a point where you believe in your own conversion. God believes in it. He wants you to believe in it. At some point you are going to have to believe in what God has done and is doing in you the way He believes in what He has done and is doing in you.

God's desire for the new creation is to be conformed to the image of Jesus. He has a way that He plans to execute this goal. What we are becoming is not up to us. This part is important. The goal of the grace that God has issued to us has already been predetermined, a people that are like His Son.

Since God has already determined the destination, meaning the place of arrival that this grace He has issued is driving all our lives, it is only fitting that He has also determined the best route to take to arrive at His predetermined destination. We would call this process discipleship.

Discipleship is the journey to discipline our lives after the pattern. The pattern is Jesus. We are being conformed to His image. In the ongoing adventure to becoming more like Jesus we are disciplining our lives to be conformed to His ways according to the work of God's grace and power that has been deposited into our lives. Grace has a mission, and becoming more like Jesus looks like something in real time.

There must come a point where you believe in your own conversion.

There is a way of life that this grace is best stewarded. Discipleship can be considered as the ongoing consistent investment into the way of life that will help to best experience and demonstrate the power of

God's grace at work within us. It can also be thought of in the terms of retraining our appetites how to be satisfied.

Your old way of life conditioned you to satisfy your life a particular way; it was normal according to your old nature. Now you are brand new. You have a new nature and so new things should be normal. This will take work. It will require effort to condition your appetites to want to want the right things.

CHAPTER FIVE

RETRAINING OUR APPETITES

Becoming implies a process of change. Becoming is transformation. The idea of becoming is that you are journeying away from what you have always known yourself to be into the substance or fulfillment of something else, something different, something new.

Those of us who are in Christ have undergone a wild metamorphosis. We are different. We have been set free from the enslavement to our old nature that was producing our old life. The tyranny of sin and self has been deconstructed. We are now alive to God, filled with His Spirit, in a beautiful union with His Son, and realigned to His purposes. This is more than a mere cosmetic surgery. This is a beautiful metamorphosis. We are a new creature.

Man needed more than a little makeup added to the exterior. Painting the outside walls was not going to bring about the desires God had. Thankfully, God had plans to change the makeup of man and not just add a little bit of makeup to him. The overhaul is powerful. The outcome is precious. The trajectory man was on has been altered, and all because **This is what the journey is all about— growing up into Him who is the head.** God chose to become a man Himself.

God becoming a man and revealing Himself in the person of Jesus has now given man the ability to become like Jesus. His Spirit, working on the inside, is what has radically brought a total reconfiguration to our nature. God is using His own life, His Spirit, jealously and continually working on the inside of us, to conform us to the image of His Son.[65]

It is important that we understand we are becoming. Let's say it one more time: we are becoming. If you have given your life to Jesus, you are on a constant journey of becoming. You should take note that we said journey. It is a process and it involves being processed. Yes, a lot happened by way of an initial experience. But that initial experience must now be walked out and developed in real time and real life. And it takes real time for us to grow up and into what God desires.

---

[65] Rom 8:29

This is what the journey is all about—growing up into Him who is the head.[66]

The way your initial experience gets walked out in real time and real life is what we would call discipleship. Whether you realize it or not, we are all becoming. We are all becoming something. For those of us who are born again, the "what" we are supposed to become is not up to us. It is up to God. He has paid the price. He has paved the way. He has provided the necessary grace and power to produce the product He desires.

If you have given your life to Jesus, you are on a constant journey of becoming.

It is all because of Him. It is all from Him. It is all by Him. And it is all back to Him. Basically, it is all about God and His purposes. Your life has been grafted into a wonderful God story. This is incredibly beautiful and should help us to better align our lives with what God is doing so God can have what it is He is after.

God has a goal for your discipleship—for you to become more like His Son. He is not looking for a people that simply mimic the behaviors of Jesus. Discipleship isn't a behavioral modification strategy

---

[66] Eph 4:15

or technique. Discipleship will absolutely affect and involve our behaviors, but it is more than that.

Behavioral modification alone will only modify what is happening on the outside, regardless of what is still alive and happening on the inside. God has done something to transform what is happening on the inside, and now because of that radical alteration our behaviors are different because we are actually changed and different.

The goal of our discipleship is a desire God has, and it is a people like His Son.

Discipleship is the continual investment into a way of life that will best help you to experience the grace God has issued to you and then best demonstrate the power of that grace in real life relationally to the people and circumstances around you. And God has a way of life that He calls us to. His way of life produces the product He desires. That is because our discipleship is unto something.

The goal of our discipleship is a desire God has, and it is a people like His Son. This is what grace works to produce in us. God wants a people that are more like His Son, and therefore our lives undergo an ongoing process of discipline—discipleship.

Grace has changed you. This change is something observable and measurable. This means people can watch you live and see the real effect the power of this grace has had on your life as you relate to people and situations. By watching you live people can measure the degree of transformation that has happened in your life.

You can communicate that change verbally, sure, but your real life should also and equally demonstrate that change. In simpler terms, what comes off your lips should also be coming off your life. Your language and lifestyle should be consistent. There shouldn't be any gap between what you know how to say and what people see.

There shouldn't be any gap between what you know how to say and what people see.

If you have been born again, you should not be the same. To imply a born-again experience is to imply the transformation into a new creature. The reality of this change is best evidenced in how you live your life. This means that you couldn't simply learn some new Christian tricks— meaning behaviors, new phrases, etc., and then think that would be the overall goal of what God is after.

No, no. God's goal is to do a lot more than just reorient things on the exterior of your life to appear to be more like Jesus. He wants to reconfigure things from the interior so all that flows out is happening because of the undeniable and powerful work taking place on the inside, from a heart level. Your effort and investment into discipleship should be helping God's grace accomplish the mission it is on.

Being conformed to the image of Jesus must look like something. It must get fleshed out. There are probably a lot of things you think it looks like. Attending services and gatherings. Singing songs. Giving in offerings. Praying. Flowing in power. Words of knowledge. Laying hands on the sick and seeing them recover and healed. The ability to give powerful and accurate prophetic words. Raise the dead.

All these attributes or activities might be attached to a life lived in and by God's Spirit, but you can do all the above-mentioned things without ever "becoming" more like Jesus. You can behave like Him and not actually become like Him. Explaining the difference is important because what God is after is important.

Jesus' power source is His nature. His character is powered by His nature, the actual DNA or substance of what He is. It is His makeup that makes Him what He is. Did Jesus flow in a powerful demonstration of the life of the Spirit? Yes, absolutely. But all of what He flowed in flowed from a powerful life source within—His nature. Here is the difference and it is what is different for us most of the time. Jesus operated in powerful gifts, but more importantly He had powerful character that it all flowed from.

Becoming more like Jesus is more about having our nature reconfigured to where we are like Him. Too many times we settle and stop short of becoming and too easily become satisfied with learning how to copy and paste certain behaviors that have piqued our interest. We flow in gifts but haven't been processed internally to where there is a real development or maturing of the transformed nature.

Discipleship is the ongoing cultivation of a way of life that best satisfies our appetites according to God's desires.

We are mature in our ability to wield gifts, yet immature when it comes to our character development. We are strong in "flowing" yet weak in "growing." We perfect the externals and hope to suppress the internals so they don't expose or disqualify us.

The power of God's grace and work in our lives by His Spirit has made us a new person. This new person has a new nature. This new nature has new appetites. Therefore, it is important that we take heed to God's prescription to the best way for this journey to be walked out. This is the ongoing journey we would call discipleship. Discipleship is the ongoing cultivation of a way of life that best satisfies our appetites according to God's desires.

Grace was not issued to you for you to do whatever you want to do with it. Which means you cannot think God will grant you great grace to live however you want to live. Grace may be for you but it is to fulfill what God desires. Grace works for God in you.

Grace may be for you but it is to fulfill what God desires.

Grace is not the entitlement for God to work for you and your demands. Grace has an agenda, and the power of that grace is working in us to keep us synchronized with its agenda. This is where discipleship becomes very important. Discipleship, not as a one-hour class once a month or even once a week, but an ongoing way of life that is consistent with its confession of Jesus as King.

Jesus sat down on the side of the mount in Matthew's gospel, chapters 5 to 7, and began to teach the people. He shared with them what Kingdom life looks like when it gets embodied on the earth. We know these chapters to be the Sermon on the Mount. Others have noted them to be the constitution of the Kingdom. These chapters are also referenced as the Beatitudes.

These are the chapters where Jesus reveals what He is like. This is where we find what the product of our discipleship journey should be producing. It is in these chapters that we can gaze into the face of Jesus and

His teaching about Kingdom life and get a glimpse of what our future quality of life in Him should look like. Jesus is giving them the road map for the life of a disciple, and this road map absolutely has a defined destination.

Consider some of the goals Jesus has for your discipleship and see if these same goals are what fill your heart. I ask, because often we have so many other ways that we attempt to determine maturity or growth. Jesus laid down some radical goals, and He wasn't timid about it.

Jesus' goals seem radical because they are utterly impossible to perfect in our own fleshly efforts, which is what it is all about—a life yielded to the work of His Spirit in us to do and make real what we could never do on our own or make real in our own carnal efforts.

Listen to some of these: spiritual poverty, mourning, meekness, transformed appetites, mercy, purity in heart and motives, peacemakers, joyfully persecuted, salt of the earth, light of the world, radical and joyful in giving and serving, radical and joyful in fasting and prayer, radical and joyful in forgiveness, simplicity, and a heart full of trust for God.[67, 68] These are Jesus' goals, but are they yours?

---

[67] See Matt 5-6

[68] Billy Humphrey, *The Culture of the Kingdom* (Kansas City, MO: Forerunner Publishing, 2009), 15, 43.

Jesus taught them what His overall goals of their transformation were to look like. His Spirit is producing a people that are not be the same as the rest of the world that surrounds them. A people radically transformed. A people that would be more like Him. In these chapters, Jesus shared with them, "This is who I am. This is what I am like, and, when I set up My life on the inside of you, this is what you will become like too."

He wasn't vague. He didn't muddy the waters to make it difficult to determine what it was He was after. As challenging as it is when we look through Matthew 5 to 7, He laid it all out simply and beautifully. Jesus has a destination for all His disciples. The pattern has been laid down and now all our lives are to be progressively conformed to that pattern.

The grace working in you should produce a certain quality of life. The quality should be in harmony with who Jesus is. The list of characteristics we look to that Paul writes in Galatians chapter 5, known as the fruit of the Spirit, is in perfect harmony with the overall vision of Kingdom life Jesus lays out in the Sermon on the Mount.

Paul said the work of the Spirit in us should be evidenced by our life now demonstrating specific qualities. These qualities will authenticate that God has done something in us. These qualities, nine in total, are love, joy, peace, patience, kindness, goodness, faithfulness, gentleness, and self-control.[69]

The fruit of the Spirit are the ingredients of a life that has been changed by God's power. These are the determiners that authenticate a powerful Kingdom life. These qualities become the measuring rod, the plumb line, for how Jesus forms His life on the inside of us. These characteristics should be the way we evaluate whether our discipleship is leading us to the correct destination or conclusion or not.

We too often evaluate growth or maturity by measurements Jesus did not use.

We too often evaluate growth or maturity by measurements Jesus did not use. We tend to qualify a person by their gifting or influence alone, and in many instances without any real knowledge of how transformed the substance of their life is.

Jesus said there would be many who would say to Him that they have prophesied, casted out devils, and raised the dead. He also said that His reply to them would be that He never knew them. It is time we come away from our eager tendencies to establish judgments based off shiny and impressive exteriors.

---

[69] Gal 5:22-23

Is a person who is super gifted impressive? Maybe. But do you want to know what is impressive to God? A transformed person. We need to be more impressed with transformed people than we are with gifted people.

Can you be both? Of course, but you know what I mean and the reference we are making here. Too many times we settle for one or the other, and because gifting builds influence, raises money, and creates visibility, we do whatever we can to better perfect our gifts and sadly, at the expense of that same intense attention on our character—the reconfiguration of the substance of who we are flowing out of a transformed nature.

We need to be more impressed with transformed people than we are with gifted people.

We can choose to set up our life however we think is best. However, it is also critical to understand that you can choose to set your life up in whatever way you think is best, but you cannot also guarantee the outcome.

Your setup will lead to a specific conclusion. You must set it up right to get what God says is right. You cannot set things up wrong and still demand the outcome that God says is right. It doesn't work that way. Although that is how many try to work it.

If we set up our life however we want, we will get the consequences of those choices. By setting our life up how we want we will get what we want, but will God get what He wants? This should be the question at some point in our journey

We must retrain our appetites to hunger after the right things.

that causes us to stop and make some serious adjustments where needed.

There are appetites attached to our old way of life. These appetites are what drove us to live the life we were living. These appetites were trained to be satisfied in specific ways. We could say that our appetites brought discipleship to our lives; our appetites discipled us. These old appetites have now received power by God's grace to be transformed. That grace has issued the verdict for these old appetites to be crucified, and then continually, and sometimes aggressively, retrained.

This process of retraining our appetites can also be called discipleship. It is very important. We must retrain our appetites to hunger after the right things, things that are in alignment with this new way of life, things God says are right.

Jesus said, "Blessed are those who hunger and thirst after righteousness, for they shall be filled."[70] Jesus knows man will hunger and thirst. That is not the issue. The issue is, what will you hunger and thirst for? One of the goals of the Holy Spirit working in you is to bring you to the place where you want what God wants. The idea is that you are hungering and thirsting after what God longs for Himself. What God wants He says is right, so it is right for you to hunger for this too.

One of the goals of the Holy Spirit working in you is to bring you to the place where you want what God wants.

David says that when you delight yourself in the Lord, He will give you the desires of your heart.[71] When God has your heart and you are wholly satisfied in Him, you want Him more than any other. When He is what you want, He gives you what to want. Your heart finds synchronization through your delighting in Him. When He knows that you want what He wants, He gives you the desires of your heart because they are His desires too. There is the experience of shared desire, a unified longing.

Righteousness cannot just be heard and then interpreted by our own desires. We must both hear it and see

---

[70] Matt 5:6
[71] Ps 37:4

it in accordance with what God is after. Righteousness is what God considers to be right according to a way of life. It is the way of life that best represents the effecting work and power of the grace that has been issued to you.

It is a way of life produced by the power God has imparted to you. It is a life that embodies the quality of God's own nature. God's character comes shining through in righteousness. It is a life that bears the image of His Son, Jesus. Righteousness is not ethereal or abstract; it is very clear and practical.

Paul mentions character in Romans 5. He speaks about it being forged and revealed through trials and suffering. With great perseverance there is a quality of life produced in us that demonstrates what God has done. He says this character should produce hope in us. A hope that

Righteousness is not ethereal or abstract; it is very clear and practical.

God is who He says He is. A hope that God has the power He says He has. A hope that He is actively working in us, and that work is resulting in what God wants here and now and then leading our lives towards the destination God has purposed for those who are born again and love His Son, eternal life.[72]

---

[72] Rom 5:2-5

Paul here says that this grace we have been given is reworking what is happening on the inside of our lives in order for the quality of life our new life now reveals can be something that is in alignment with the desires God has. Paul would call this character. This character is the real substance of our life that is best evidenced as we live our lives in relation to others and circumstances. And, according to Paul, suffering and trials are something that should be celebrated because of the intentional tool they become in assisting to better form in us what it is God is after.

This character, or this righteousness, should be understood as a certain quality of life that is the byproduct of God's grace having its desired effect in us. It is not verbal communication alone. It can be articulated but must be demonstrated for the authenticity of it to be real. These qualities revealed through and by this quality of life are what God says is right.

The ingredients of character God is after forming in those who love His Son is what He says is right. This is because there is a way of life God longs to have demonstrated in the earth. A way that best reveals and represents Him. A way of life that gives off a witness.

Jesus said we would receive power when the Holy Spirit comes upon us to be His witnesses.[73] He first

---

[73] Acts 1:8

lived it out Himself. Now, He is the pattern. He longs to have that same life, that same quality of life, lived out by those He is forming into His image. Our being conformed to the image of Jesus is about our lives being conformed to a particular way of life that demonstrates the character and power of God in real time, regardless of the context our life is put in.

We should have a longing within us for God to form His life in us and for that life to be demonstrated to the world around us.

We know what God wants, and so it is right that we hunger and thirst for righteousness. We should have a longing within us for God to form His life in us and for that life to be demonstrated to the world around us. We should be hungry for what God wants. We should have a thirst within that can only be quenched by God's desires becoming manifested in us and others.

There is a churning deep within, a hunger, for God to perform and perfect that which He has poured out His own Spirit to see produced. A people of powerful character must emerge. A people of supernatural character must come to the surface. A people radically transformed into the image of Jesus through the power of God's grace.

Paul's list of observables and measurables are love, joy, peace, patience, kindness, goodness, faithfulness, gentleness, and self-control. Jesus' list of observables and measurables are spiritual poverty, mourning, meekness, spiritual hunger, mercy, purity in heart, being a peacemaker, willingness to be persecuted for righteousness, giving, serving, prayer, forgiveness, fasting, living simply, a heart full of trust for God.

We need discipleship that better helps us to know what God wants.

Are any of these items on your list? When you think of the life God longs to form within you, do you consider any of these things Paul and/or Jesus have included?

Too many times we have our own idea of what we think God wants. Our list gets compiled with our own desires. We form our list of wants and then we hope, wish, and pray that God is going to want what we want. We need discipleship that better helps us to know what God wants.

Upon realizing what He wants, we must then be given over to a consistent way of life that will better set us up to experience the grace He has issued for what He wants. If we want to fully demonstrate the power of that grace, we must be fully given over to the way He has said it is best stewarded.

There are certain ingredients that must be a part of our life for the agenda of God's grace in our lives to best be accomplished. These ingredients are like beautiful and powerful tools that will assist in the accomplishment of the agenda of what God's grace is jealous to fulfill. We will take the next couple of chapters to discuss some of these ingredients.

CHAPTER SIX

BEHOLDING THE LORD IN THE WORD AND WORSHIP

We must be intentional about discipleship. We are called to first become disciples of Jesus; and then out of our own discipleship experience and journey we are to make disciples of others. Making disciples is instrumental to the overall mission God is on.

Jesus, when talking with His disciples, said, "Go, therefore, and make disciples of all nations."[74] The idea is that disciples make disciples. Not just some disciples, but all disciples. All disciples should be making disciples. At least that is what Jesus thinks, and if that is what He thinks, that is what we should think too.

Discipleship must be intentional because God has an intentional goal for our discipleship. This means it

---

[74] Matt 28:19

would be best that we align our lives with the path that best produces the product God desires. Which means we cannot assume that all our own ideas about what discipleship should

Discipleship must be intentional because God has an intentional goal for our discipleship.

look like or how best it can be lived out are relevant to what God wants.

God is after something. The "what" that God is after has a "way" that God knows it can best be accomplished. We must align our hearts and lives to His way if we want our lives to become what He wants.

The word discipleship comes from the word disciple, and the word disciple comes from the word discipline. Discipline is an interesting word. It can be defined as the constant exercise used to bring to a state of order and obedience by training or control. It is an intentional and continual investment into a process that should produce a desired goal. It can be thought of in the terms of a way of life strategically arranged to best bring about the delivery on what is desired.

Disciples discipline themselves to best align their hearts and lives to the way God has said is best, believing that what God wants will be formed in their lives by the power of His Spirit working in and with them. These are disciples. Real disciples are not doing their own thing; they are given over to doing the Jesus thing.

Doing their own thing is not what will produce the product God desires. He wants a people that look like Jesus, and thus that is why we must do more and more of the Jesus thing—the Jesus thing being a reference to intentional and ongoing discipleship that will conform us to the image of the pattern, the man Jesus.

Thankfully God has not left us to our own devices to best fulfill His purposes. There are very real and specific practical tools God has invited us to participate in that are aids in what it is He is after. These tools are beautiful. These tools are a means that serve God's purposes. These tools are not necessarily goals in and of themselves, but help to fulfill the goal God has of making a people conformed to the image of His Son.

> **We must align our hearts and lives to His way if we want our lives to become what He wants.**

We will talk briefly about some of these tools. I have written about some of them extensively in other books, so I don't want to restate things that have been further expounded upon in other resources. But it is needed here to bring formation to the conversation as to the necessity of these tools in our lives and the purpose they serve to make us what God desires.

THE WORD

"The Word of God is powerful. It is living and active, sharper than any two-edged sword, even penetrating as far as the division of soul and spirit, of both joints and marrow, and able to judge the thoughts and intentions of the heart."[75]

God has gone to great lengths to reveal Himself the way that He wants to be known. Our discipleship journey must include the Word of God. The Bible is the Word of God. It is infallible. It is inspired by God's Spirit that moved men to write. It is to be taken seriously and consumed regularly. It must become our delight, our meditation day and night.[76] We must delight in it and not forget it.[77]

The Bible helps to familiarize our hearts with who God is and what He is like. This is very important. God has gone to great lengths to reveal Himself. He has gone to great lengths to reveal Himself the way that He wants to be known. Hear that again. The way that He Himself wants to be known.

I know there are many that come up with their own idea of who and what they want God to be. This

---

[75] Heb 4:12, NASB
[76] Ps 1:2
[77] Ps 119:16

is utter nonsense, and the foolishness of this will all be fully revealed on that great day when God comes to abide in the midst of His people forever.[78]

This we can know for sure; at the end of the age, the moment that all of time comes to an end by the returning of King Jesus, God will be exactly who He has revealed Himself to be all along. There will be no surprise as to who God is or what He will be like. At least there shouldn't be because of how intentional He has been through the revealing of Himself in His Word.

The Scriptures help to reveal God. They do not fully contain Him, as if to assume that the Bible is all there is to Him. No, they reveal beautiful things about God. God has not limited Himself to what He has disclosed about Himself in His Word.

He has chosen to reveal certain things about who He is and what He is like so we can better come to know Him. But that should not then allow us to feel that we could limit the power or the potential of the Word of God in our lives. Especially since the Word of God is one of the primary ways God has chosen to allow Himself to be known. God wants to be known. Part of the way He has chosen to allow man to familiarize his heart with knowing Him is through His Word.

---

[78] Rev 21:3-4

We need the influence of the Scriptures by the Spirit in our journey of becoming a disciple. Notice I didn't just say the Word alone. The letter alone kills, but the Spirit gives life.[79] It is too easy to think that if we just memorize a bunch of Bible verses we are fulfilling our duty to God. This is not all that God is after.

We can articulate revelation, but God wants our lives to become a revelation as the Word gets embodied.

Scripture memorization has its place. But what is more ultimate than just simply memorizing the Scriptures is allowing what is gleaned in the Scriptures to pierce our hearts and produce what God is after in us, which is the image of His Son. We can articulate revelation, but God wants our lives to become a revelation as the Word gets embodied. The Word became flesh and dwelt amongst us.[80]

What we read in the Bible should help to form our lives to look more like Jesus. Reading should produce forming. How? Because the Bible helps us to better familiarize ourselves with what God is like.

This is one of the points. The Bible is not just a story for the sake of historical or entertainment-driven purposes alone. No, the Word is alive. All of what we

---

[79] 2 Cor 3:6
[80] John 1:14

have is written and serves a purpose to better help us lean into the knowledge of God through what God has chosen to reveal of Himself.

The stories throughout the Scriptures give us insight as to how God has revealed Himself as He has chosen to interact with men and circumstances throughout the ages. They tell us very important details that are to be gleaned so we can better know Him.

None of it is accidental. It is all being communicated because there are things about God that He longs to communicate to us as we open our hearts to the influence of His Spirit.

We learn God's character as we study what He has revealed throughout the Scriptures. This is important because it tells us what God is like. He has not bound Himself to being like what we want Him to be like. He is free from that. He is not insecure. So He does not have to rush into all of our ideas of Him to satisfy what we want Him to be like. No, He feels no pressure for that whatsoever. He is free to be Himself and is in fact very comfortable with who He is and what He is like. He is not insecure.

By gaining a better idea of what God is like we can better understand His goals for the formation of our lives. He wants a people that are more like Him. He is not looking for the best version of you; He wants you to be conformed to the image of His Son. This is the goal, and He is very committed to what He wants. He has issued power to you to transform your nature and character to that which is like His Son.

He is not looking for the best version of you; He wants you to be conformed to the image of His Son.

It is important that we become students of the Word because it is here that God has revealed what He wants to be known about His character. In the Word is where we can learn what God is like. Another thing we learn in the Word is what it is God wants. We learn what He is like and we learn what He wants.

The story of the Scriptures reveals God and His desires. It is not just a self-help book. It is not a place where we cherry-pick our favorite Bible verses to massage them into our own self-generated desires and demands. All throughout the Bible we get a glimpse of God and a glimpse of what it is He is after. We learn His ways and we learn what He wants.

Through the Word He has chosen to reveal Himself and His desires. This is precious and cannot be taken lightly. It is too easy to approach the Word with ourselves in mind. All the culture around us is constantly bombarding us, attempting to disciple us and condition us to believe that all that matters is what we want.

The "I" in life has taken center stage, and the rest of the surrounding pieces and circumstances are all supposed to support and help serve whatever it is the "I" feels it wants. But this is very difficult to maintain when we approach the Scriptures the way we are supposed to. In the Scriptures we learn that all of life is not about the "I" in our lives; it is about the Great I Am. Life is about God.

God has invited us into His story. He has chosen to make us members of His family. He has given us His own Spirit, His life, so we will live with Him forever, ruling alongside of His Son as a faithful companion. This is God's story. This is what God wants.

In the Scriptures we learn that all of life is not about the "I" in our lives; it is about the Great I Am.

As we come to the Word with the right heart posture, we can gain better insight and traction for our lives pertaining to who God is, what He is like, what He ultimately wants, and how all of that should radically align our lives to Him and His purposes. This is what the Word should accomplish in our hearts and lives.

"Man shall not live by bread alone, but by every word that proceeds from the mouth of God."[81] We

---

[81] Matt 4:4, NKJV

must live by the Word. It must form our lives. It must inform and form our convictions. It must provide for us the necessary road map as to how we will all bring navigation to our lives and the circumstances that will confront us and demand that we be something in response. The Word must have its work in us for us to be what God desires. We must consume it. It must become us.

The Word must have its work in us for us to be what God desires.

WORSHIP

Worship is one of the elements of our devotional walk with God that has been misinterpreted for quite some time. It has been misaligned. Worship is not a performance. Worship is not a concert. Worship is not an industry. Worship is not a vibe. Worship is not even necessarily about music at all or song lyrics alone. The true definition of worship is none of these things. Worship is one of the ingredients in our obedience to God that must be adjusted and brought back to its proper position and intentions.

The first mention of worship is found in Genesis chapter 22. Abram has received a very difficult word from God. He knows that the son he loves, the one through whom God has promised to fulfill every word about how his personal destiny is going to come, he is supposed to take him and sacrifice him upon a mount that God will reveal to him. Abram rises early the next morning to fulfill this word. He begins journeying with Isaac to the place that God would show him where he will obey the word that he knows God gave him and there upon the mount slay his son in the presence of God. This is wild.

I have received some difficult words over the course of my life, but none to the degree of intensity that the Bible says Abram received. I have five children and I don't honestly know if I would wake up early the next morning and rush off to obey the word like Abram did. I'm just being honest. Sacrificing one of my kids is not high at all on the priority list. However, when Abram gets to the bottom of the mount, the place where he knew his obedience would ultimately need to be followed through with, he said to those at the foot of the mount, "Stay here, and the boy and I will go the top of the mount to worship."[82]

Abram knew what God said and what he had to do about it. He had to walk out one of the toughest yeses of his entire life. In doing so, he had to trust God's leadership in his life. Abram had to take inventory of his situation and make an intentional decision to go all

---

[82] Gen 22:1-5

in with God, holding nothing back in his own heart that would affect the yes to God that God was asking him for. Abram chose God, gave Him his wholehearted yes, and obeyed Him, no matter the consequences. This is true worship.

The Bible intentionally creates the idea of worship as God being worthy of any yes He asks for.

Worship is the yes that comes out of your heart and off your life as you live it out to God. Worship is the yes that erupts from the inside when you know that God has revealed Himself and revealed His desires to you. Worship is the yes that you give to God. This is what Abram had.

Abram was a worshipper. Abram didn't learn how to worship while resisting a yes in his heart to God. Abram's yes in his heart to God is what authenticated him as a worshipper. It is important that we return to a true definition of worship so the implications of worship can create the impact in our hearts and lives it is intended to.

Worship is intended to be directed toward God. He alone is the One worthy to be worshipped. Worship is the yes that comes out of our heart and off our lives as we live that yes in the direction of God Himself and the obeying of His desires. It can include songs at times, but it is not limited to songs alone.

I don't know if Abram was singing as he was climbing the mount that day; the Bible doesn't say. I am glad the Bible doesn't say anything about songs or music or musicians when worship is first mentioned. I am glad the Bible intentionally creates the idea of worship as God being worthy of any yes He asks for. There is a real tension this scenario creates, as we all must consider what our yes looks like to the things we know God has said to us individually.

I am glad there is nothing about Abram having one fast song and then transitioning to two slow songs before he took Isaac up as the offering on the mount. This is obviously not to poke fun about the structuring of services with worship. But there are too many that sing songs on Sunday and then don't live out a yes to God Monday to Saturday. If what you sing on Sunday doesn't change the way you offer up a yes to God every other day, then maybe you need to evaluate if you are worshipping, or better than that, who you are worshipping.

There are too many that sing songs on Sunday and then don't live out a yes to God Monday to Saturday.

We too often center life on ourselves. This contaminates our idea of worship. We judge worship experiences. We issue grades to worship leaders and their abilities. We create preferences of styles, flavors, genres, etc., and then we approach our idea of worship with a predetermined posture we enter into so that something on the inside of us can be satisfied.

God alone is the only person that can be worshipped and still be Himself.

We say things like, "I didn't really like the songs we sang today." Or, "You know, I wasn't really feeling the way that worship went today." Or something as simple sounding as the question, "How was worship today?"

All these thoughts, comments, and questions reveal a greater issue than just the answers to these things. What is ultimately revealed is that we are more accustomed to worshipping ourselves than we are God, Himself. We center all our life on us and then bring this very same mindset into our worship experience. We think everything in life orbits around our desires and waits to satisfy our every felt need. This is a problem.

The problem with this is we were not created with a capacity to handle being worshipped. God alone is the only person in the universe worthy to be worshipped. God alone is the only person that can be worshipped and still be Himself. He is unchanged by worship. Is He worthy of worship? Absolutely and indefinitely.

However, His worth is not created by or limited to our worship.

This is the point. God is who He is. He is unchanging. He is eternally the same. He is constant. We don't worship Him so He can change. He is not affected by worship this way. He can be worshipped constantly, and amid constant worship, beautifully and consistently remain Himself. We do not worship Him to make Him something He is not already.

In our worship, we are responding to the beauty and worthiness of God, and it is not changing Him; it is changing us. Worship is about adoration and transformation. You become what you behold. The becoming is in the beholding. Therefore, we are not meant to be worshipped; it changes us.

We do not have the capacity to be worshipped and remain unchanged. We are not supposed to be the object of worship. More plainly put, we are not to be the featured attraction in our heart—God is. He is supposed to take center stage.

God knows one of the best things He can do for us is to reveal Himself to us. In the revealing of Himself to us we are invited to worship Him. Worship is the proper response to His beauty and worth.

Do you realize that everything that sees God rightly responds to Him in the only appropriate way— worship? Elders, angels, creatures, seraphim, and saints, all worship God.[83] Even rocks cry out and praise has been ordained out of the mouths of babes.[84] God's worth places a demand for worship, though He Himself does not demand it out of some felt need.

The satisfaction of the heart will always be revealed through the pursuit of our life.

He is infinitely secure and understands that one of the ways His purposes are best served in our hearts and lives is through worship, and not the worship of ourselves, but worship directed to Him through the revealing of Himself to us.

We are changed through worship. This is one of the reasons worship must be seen correctly in our ongoing discipleship process. We experience transformation through worship. God knows this. He understands that through His invitation to worship Him He is inviting us to become more like Him.

Our becoming can be found in what we are beholding. When we behold God in worship, we are invited into a process of transformation that will result in our being transformed into what it is we have been privileged to behold. If we are to become more like God, God must be our object of worship.

---

[83] See Eze 1; Isa 6; Rev 4, 5, 19
[84] See Luke 19:40; Ps 8:2

The opposite is equally true. It is the reason it must be mentioned. When we become the object of our worship, our self-interests, rather than God's interests, are what get magnified. This is a slippery slope and a dangerous cliff to dance on. When our self-interests are what gets magnified, we become the embodiment of our self-interests rather than God's interests.

You see it all the time. People begin to change. They begin to be transformed. They start to embody what has captivated their heart. The substance of their life begins to be saturated with whatever it is that has become their ultimate obsession.

When the pursuit of God is real in your life and you legitimately carry a desire to live out a wholehearted yes to God, it overtakes your life.

The satisfaction of the heart will always be revealed through the pursuit of our life. There is no way around this. And when our heart has been satisfied by something other than God, we will pursue the supplier of our satisfaction with all our heart, and there we will set up an altar of worship, many times without ever fully realizing what is happening along the way.

God alone should be our ultimate obsession. God alone should be what captivates and satisfies our heart. When the pursuit of God is real in your life and you legitimately carry a desire to live out a wholehearted yes to God, it overtakes your life.

From that place you will find yourself authenticated as a worshipper, and not just one that has memorized a few songs, but one that also realizes there is not a real intention on living the lyrics. We must desire to live the lyrics. Jesus said there were those who praised Him with their lips, but their hearts were far from Him.[85]

We want to be known as those who are living it and singing it, not those who are singing it and not living it. Songs should rise from our hearts. We should sing a new song to the Lord.[86] There is zero issue with singing. In fact, singing is one of the beautiful ways we can cultivate the power of the Word that is in us and in our midst as a people.

Paul encouraged the believers in Colossae this way, "Let the word of Christ richly dwell within you as you teach and admonish one another with all wisdom, and as you sing psalms, hymns, and spiritual songs with gratitude in your hearts to God."[87]

We should sing. God Himself sings.[88] We just need to adjust our lens so we don't assume our entire worship to God is possible through hollowly throwing

---

[85] Matt 15:8
[86] Ps 96:1, 98:1; Isa 42:10
[87] Col 3:16, BSB
[88] Zeph 3:17

our singing at God without the corresponding living. Our singing should rise out of what we are living.

When God is our interest, we will worship Him. When we worship Him, He will have His way in us. God's rule and government is always associated with worship. In times when men were caught up to see into the heavenly throne room of God there has always been a company that surround God that responded to Him the only way that is eternally appropriate—with worship!

Worship and government go together. God is enthroned upon the praises of His people.[89] Through worship, God can establish His throne in your heart. What is real in the heavens becomes very real to us in our hearts as we respond to the beauty and worth of God in worship.

When God's government is established in our heart through worship, we will follow Him in obedience. The yes God desires will be His when we give ourselves to worship Him as He reveals Himself to us. The worshipful response of yes will flow from the heart brought subject to God's rule through worship. Another way to say this is—one of the ways we worship God is with our yes. You worship Him with your yes.

---

[89] Ps 22:3

One of the ways you can love Him well and know you are loving Him well is with your yes. Jesus said those that really loved Him would be those willing to obey Him.[90] Obedience is an evidence and determiner of love. One of God's love languages is obedience. He feels loved by your yes.

Therefore, Abram couldn't have sung a song and then expected God to exempt him from following through with the word that He gave him. It's the same for you. Do not be deceived into believing that if you can just memorize the right songs, God will exempt you from living in response to what He has revealed to you. The ultimate evidence of a true worshipper is a softer heart and a greater yes.

One of God's love languages is obedience. He feels loved by your yes.

"God, You rule my life. I have been brought subject to Your government. I don't want my own way anymore; I will follow You. Say whatever You want to say. Do whatever You know needs to be done. I am all Yours. You can have my whole yes." This is the song of the worshipper. This should be our song. This would have been the song Abram sang as he was climbing the mount that day to kill his son in the presence of God.

---

[90] John 14:15

Worship changes us. Worship should transform our lives and the desires of our lives. In response to God's beauty and worth, He has issued the invitation to serve His desires in us through worship. He knows that what is best for us is to see Him, worship Him, and then allow the power of His Spirit to work in us and free us from all that resists us from offering the yes to Him that He longs for.

Our worship doesn't change God; it changes us. God issues the invitation for people to worship Him so He can transform their lives. He serves us through our worship of Him when we respond to Him. This doesn't make any natural sense. It is mind-blowing. But our God is mind-blowing. The greater He reveals Himself to our hearts

Worship should transform our lives and the desires of our lives.

should produce a greater awe and wonder and drive us to deeper and more places of worship, and when those times are accompanied by songs, praise God!

Worship must be a part of our process of discipleship. In beholding the Lord, we are invited to worship Him. This proper response to His beauty and worth purifies every other pursuit in our life as God is exalted above every other and takes His rightful place in our heart. This ongoing journey continually brings us to the consideration of subjection, and God can rule in our hearts and over our lives. Where His government is established, the reality of His Kingship is experienced. He is King, and He reigns, and it is very real, but He longs for it to be very real in us.

In our next chapter we will look at two more beautiful components of our discipleship process God uses to fulfill His agenda in our lives. None of these ingredients are a life unto themselves but rather are powerfully interdependent so they all feed off and into one another. In other words, we need the whole pie; you don't settle or choose to be satisfied with whatever individual piece is your preference.

CHAPTER SEVEN

BEHOLDING THE LORD IN FASTING AND PRAYER

FASTING

I have written two volumes about fasting. There will be more to come—but we will save that for a later time. I would strongly encourage you to consider these volumes to reorient your perspective on fasting as a lifestyle. We can begin by saying that fasting is a gift from God, and it is necessary in the life of a believer. Fasting is one of the needed ingredients for us to behold Him and be conformed to His image.

Fasting should be thought of in terms of intimacy. This may be tough, especially if you have ever had a difficult time fasting. I think we can all agree that fasting is not always easy. And that's okay; it is not meant to be. It is hard. It is also incredibly rewarding, and the prize always eclipses the pain.

My life in fasting radically changed when I felt the Holy Spirit ask me a question. We all have these moments. You sense an inner voice. You weren't trying to work something up. You didn't have your thoughts pushed in a particular direction. And then, there it is. Suddenly there is an inner speaking. I felt the Holy Spirit ask me, "Will you love Him this way?" Here is where fasting gets viewed through the lens of intimacy. Jesus feels loved by our obedience.

There are things you can do in practical ways with your life that can move the heart of Jesus.

Jesus said those that love Him would obey Him.[91] Obeying Jesus is loving Jesus. Or to say it another way, to obey Him is to love Him. Have you ever considered that Jesus can feel loved? He can be moved. He is a person, a real person. He became a man. As a man, He is a person. As a person, He has a personality. There are real emotions to Him, and they can be moved. They can be moved positively and they can also be moved negatively. Has this ever crossed your mind? To think there are things you can do in practical ways with your life that can move the heart of Jesus? This is a wild thought and that's okay; it is supposed to be.

[91] John 14:15

Fasting is one of the ways we obey Jesus. It is one of the beautiful ways we get to love Him and move His heart. Have you ever thought that when you turn away from food in the place of fasting that it moves the heart of Jesus? Why? Not because He enjoys watching you suffer through it. Not because He has some weird affinity towards you struggling while on a fast. Not at all.

The issue always seems to get more focused on what we are turning away from. This is where our perspective needs altered. Why are we always so focused on what we are refraining from? Could it be because we are too preoccupied with ourselves? Maybe. And maybe that is part of the point in fasting. I would say so.

Fasting is about refraining from lesser satisfactions to make room for more ultimate satisfaction.

We tend to immediately and always think about losing out on food rather than on gaining more of Jesus. We think about the things we will lack rather than all of what there is to be gained. Fasting is not about losing; it is about gaining.

Fasting is about refraining from lesser satisfactions to make room for more ultimate satisfaction. You turn away from others to turn to Him in a more intentional way. You are offloading other things from your appetites and attention to be more available to Him. Giving more of yourself to Jesus sometimes looks like something very practical. Fasting is part of the process that helps to make it very real.

There is something about the addiction to His presence that gets restored in times of fasting.

Jesus said, in Matthew chapter 9 that when He would be taken from His followers, then they would fast.[92] This was in response to being questioned by the disciples of John. The contrast was the disciples of John and the Pharisees.

It is to be noted that the Pharisees had a practice of fasting two days a week. Seems special, right? They fasted two days a week out of performance and not out of pursuit. Their efforts were fueled by religious obligation and not intimate devotion. It was the obligatory effort required to maintain the upkeep of their whitewashed exterior—for which they were later rebuked for by Jesus.[93]

However, part of the idea here that Jesus was communicating is that there would come a time when His followers would no longer have Him the way they had grown accustomed to. In those days, when the

---

[92] Matt 9:15
[93] Matt 23:25-28

nearness of His person, His presence, was taken up from them, then they would fast.

There is something about the addiction to His presence that gets restored in times of fasting. When the bridegroom is taken from them, then they will fast. Jesus believes that part of our fuel for fasting should be the consideration of His absence.

The absence of Jesus should not be okay with us. Is it okay with you? He is not here, and things should not be okay. Regardless of how well you decorate your life with successes or material things, you should not be able to satisfy your heart fully in this life. Why? Because the bridegroom has been taken up from us.

Jesus believes that part of our fuel for fasting should be the consideration of His absence.

His desire is to be with His people. It is what His heart is on fire for. His heart fire is fueled by the desire for the bride, His inheritance, His reward. The reward of His sufferings is a people, from every tribe, nation, and tongue.[94] It is His longing to be with His people. But is it our longing to be with Him? This is something we must ask ourselves and allow the much-needed confrontation to take place in our appetites.

---

[94] See Dan 7:14; John 17:24; Rev 5:9; Rev 7:9

The Bible says that towards the end of the age, before the return of Jesus, the Spirit and the bride will have a unified cry.[95] There will be a longing that fills the bride that has been burning with the Spirit. This cry will not be for a political party to win out over another. This cry will not be for a social justice movement. This cry will not be for material wealth, success, fame, or even worldly power and/or influence. None of those things are going to be what matters most before the return of Jesus.

The Bible says that the Spirit and the bride will say, "Come, Lord Jesus."[96] The bride will have a singular desire, King Jesus. Every other will be sifted from the heart and request. All other lesser lovers will have fallen off of the radar and the sights of the bride will be honed in on the bridegroom. The desire for the bridegroom will increase and every other will decrease. Maranatha will be what burns in the heart and comes off the lips of the bride.

If we take what Jesus said in Matthew chapter 9 seriously and practically and let Him say what He is saying without massaging it into something more palatable for what we want or think is best, then what He is saying is that fasting will be fueled by absence;

---

[95] See Rev 22:17
[96] Rev 22:17

and fasting fueled by absence will help to increase our capacity to house this Maranatha cry.

He is not here, and everything is not okay. Our heart should be on fire with what fuels the fire in His heart—union. Our hearts burn to be reunited with our bridegroom King! An appetite for the return of Jesus will be the dominant theme for the bride before He comes again.

Fasting is a wonderful tool that digs deep into our lives and exposes what really satisfies our hungers.

Fasting is one of the crucibles that examines and exposes our appetites. It reveals what we search for whenever an appetite in our life demands to be satisfied. The issue is not that we have these appetites. We have all been born with certain appetites. The appetites in and of themselves are not wrong. The issue is who, what, or where we go to satisfy the variety of cravings that arise from within.

At times, we are not even aware of these things until we get into a fast. You must remember: fasting is a means to an end, not an end. It is a tool. Fasting is a wonderful tool that digs deep into our lives and exposes what really satisfies our hungers.

There is much happening whenever we turn away from the table and turn to Jesus. Jesus said, "When you fast . . ."[97] The idea of "when" is very different than "if." It should not be debatable. Every believer should have the practice of fasting incorporated as a

If it is important to Jesus, it should be important to us, and fasting is important to Jesus.

lifestyle, a lifestyle meaning an ongoing effort to discipline our lives this way.

If it is important to Jesus, it should be important to us, and fasting is important to Jesus. Fasting is a part of the encouragements in Matthew chapter 6 that can be referenced as the three "when you dos." In Matthew chapter 6 you have when you give, when you pray, and when you fast.[98]

Many only focus on what to do in the place of fasting, and that is somewhat okay. But only focusing on "what" will not sustain the lifestyle practice for the long haul. The "what" must be informed and inspired by the "why." The "why" leads us to the "who," and that's the point. Otherwise, fasting gets derailed from the intended purpose and turns into a self-satisfying, agenda-oriented issue.

It becomes more about what I want, what I want God to do, the items on my list I target during a fast, and so forth. This is not to say that at times there are

---

[97] Matt 6:16
[98] Matt 6:2, 6,16

not extraordinary things God longs to see accomplished through us and for us during times of our obedient investments into fasting. There absolutely are. However, we are not fundamentally motivated by the immediate and material things of this life as proper fuel for fasting.

Many times it is not until we get into a fast that the Spirit can clearly reveal to us the "why" we are doing what we are doing. Our lives easily become insulated to God's voice through a host of other satisfactions. We are totally oblivious to His desire. We don't have an attention to hear Him because of all the ways we satisfy the tug and tension in our hearts. It creates real issues over time.

Fasting helps to expose these different attempts to insulate our hearts and satisfy our lives with other things than God Himself.

This is one of the many reasons why fasting is such a beautiful gift. It helps to expose these different attempts to insulate our hearts and satisfy our lives with other things than God Himself. For some it is entertainment. Others it is their career and the passion associated with work. For others, it is relational connections. To others it is material things, shopping, and constantly consuming and acquiring stuff. The well we run to can vary person to person, but the root issue is the same—the desire to be satisfied by something, someone, or somewhere other than God Himself.

Too much of our preoccupation and our priorities get consumed by other things when God Himself is not where we have found our ultimate satisfaction. Fasting helps here. It helps to recenter the preoccupation of our hearts and the affection of our lives on Jesus. Not just in some abstract way that gets satisfied by the right language, but in the very real and practical adjustments that come out of times of fasting. Our lives begin to line up and exclaim, "I love Him!" "He means everything to me!" "I want Him more than anything else!"

Too much of our preoccupation and our priorities get consumed by other things when God Himself is not where we have found our ultimate satisfaction.

In fasting we find the turning over of our attention, affection, and appetites to Jesus as King. You must be aware of what does it for you. Fasting helps here. Fasting exposes our allegiances. It helps to identify the substance of what really satisfies the inner longings. It touches what sets our affections ablaze.

PRAYER

Prayer, in a simple way, is about dependency. Prayer is about dependency because it reveals the believed source of our life and its efforts. Prayer identifies where our anchor has been put down. The man who is unwilling to pray is the man who has chosen to lean more fully on himself than on God. David writes, "My soul waits in silence for God alone; From Him comes my salvation. He alone is my rock and my salvation, my stronghold; I will not be greatly shaken."[99]

In another psalm, David's heart erupts when he pens, "My soul clings to You; Your right hand takes hold of me."[100] In these verses we find the beauty of prayer—

Prayer is about dependency, and not dependency in or on ourselves, but dependency on God and God alone.

the ongoing relational experience of clinging to God. Prayer is about dependency, and not dependency in or on ourselves, but dependency on God and God alone.

Prayer is one of the beautiful ways to behold the Lord. Jesus instructed us to go into our closet, close the door behind us, and our Father, who sees us in

---

[99] Ps 62:1-2, NASB
[100] Ps 63:8, NASB

secret, will hear us and then reward us in public."[101] The reward of prayer is God Himself. We come to Him for Him.

When we come to Him for Him, we never leave disappointed because He always makes good on giving of Himself to those who **The reward of prayer** believe that He is and dili- **is God Himself.** gently seek after Him. He is the rewarder of those that diligently seek Him.[102] When we seek, we find. When we knock, the door is opened to us. When we ask, we receive. God longs to be known, and He desires to be found by those who come to Him for Him.

Prayer is not a waste of time. Martin Luther is quoted as saying, "If I fail to spend two hours in prayer each morning, the devil gets the victory throughout the day."[103] He is also remembered for saying, "I have so much to do today that I'm going to need to spend three hours in prayer to be able to get it all done."[104]

Do not get so caught up on the amount of time he refers to that you miss the whole point. Luther did

---

[101] Matt 6:6

[102] See Heb 11:6

[103] *Beggars All: Reformation & Apologetics*, "Luther: I have so much to do that I shall have to spend the first three hours in prayer," https://beggarsallreformation.blogspot.com/2009/07/luther-i-have-so-much-to-do-that-i.html.

[104] *Quote Catalog*, Martin Luther Quote, https://quotecatalog.com/quote/martin-luther-i-have-so-much-MpxPPyp/.

not only find God to be a necessary resource in case of emergency. God was not the "in case of emergency, break glass" solution to him. No, no. God was more than a lifeline in times of desperation or trouble; God was his source. He was central to life itself.

Do you see God as your source? If not, then you will not find it necessary to pray. Prayer is essential for those who realize that the quality of their life experience is dependent upon God, for it is in the place of prayer that our hearts are confronted and satisfied.

We are confronted with all our tendencies to want independence rather than dependence upon God. And with God Himself satisfying the deep places within us, we come to learn all the others we turn to in attempt to find temporary fulfillment. To whom God has become life, they will

Prayer is essential for those who realize that the quality of their life experience is dependent upon God.

joyfully and continually give themselves to prayer. They will cling to Him, and ever ask for the strengthening of their grip by His grace.

My soul waits upon God alone. This is a tremendous statement. Especially with all the cultural conditioning that is radically opposed to the idea of us having to wait for anything at all. Everything that we want, we are told, we should be able to have, and have it on demand most times.

Everything for us and to us has grown in the immediacy of how accessible it is. And if we are not careful, we very easily become deeply impacted or discipled by our culture and it then affects the way we come to God.

Prayer is the ongoing relational experience of repeatedly realizing our utter dependency upon and desperate need for God and God alone.

We are impatient. Nobody enjoys waiting for anything. Frustration builds whenever there are not immediate answers given, resolutions provided, doors opened, dots connected. There is something about time that creates tension.

We realize that time is not waiting around for any of us. We feel as if there is much to be responsible for, and for most of what we feel responsible for, time has a great influence on all those items. So the idea of spending significant amounts of time praying in many cases is perceived to be a waste of time. Yet with all our propensity to impatience, David waits, and he waits on God alone.

David is not waiting for answers. He is not waiting for doors to open. He is not waiting for breakthrough or provision. He is waiting for God. Prayer is the ongoing relational experience of repeatedly realizing our utter dependency upon and desperate need for God and God alone. David waitis because he has been broken by God in the place of waiting.

We bring so much stuff into our time with the Lord mostly for reasons that we think are okay and good. We bring all our stuff. All our lists of things we want to see God do, most of which has a unique way of eclipsing our ability to meet with Him purely. It obscures our view of Him because we have already predetermined the basis upon which He must meet us—our lists and stuff.

When frustrated by life we carry all those aggravations to God, but often not with pure intent to cast our burden upon Him because we realize He cares for us.[105] Rather out of a lack of being able to control our own lives we carry to God all our irritations with Him and how He is not performing for us the way we would desire. We try and enforce our will in the place of prayer rather than becoming beautifully bridled by the Lord as we are overwhelmed by His loving intentions toward us.

Bridle is a term used for strong and wild horses. It is the process of being able to rest upon them. They first must be broken of the strength of their own will. The strength of the horse and its current felt demands

---

[105] Ps 55:22; 1 Pet 5:7

tend to make it very difficult for the rider to rest. The rider doesn't want the horse to lose its might; he just knows that it needed to be broken of its independence so its strength can be channeled correctly.

More than doing things for you, God wants to be all to you.

This is the idea. Too many of us are the wild horse in the place of coming to God. We come on our own terms. We buck. We wrestle. We demand our own way. God waits. He loves. He keeps giving of Himself. He knows His influence is greater; He will hopefully win out in the end. He desires this because more than doing things for you, God wants to be all to you.

To behold Him, we must come to see Him as He longs to reveal Himself. When we predetermine who we want Him to be, it makes it tough to see Him as He is. As He is sets our hearts free. As He is transforms our lives. Beholding Him as He is makes provision for us to become like what He has graciously allowed to be revealed of Himself.

Prayer is an essential part of this process. Seeing Him constantly in the place of prayer provides the necessary glimpse and grace to be transformed into the image of what the Spirit beautifully unveils to our hearts. I'll leave us with the words of Paul that seem very appropriate here. "But we all, with unveiled faces, looking as in a mirror at the glory of the Lord, are being transformed into the image from glory to glory, just as from the Lord, the Spirit."[106]

---

[106] 2 Cor 3:18, NASB

CHAPTER EIGHT

BEHOLDING THE LORD IN COMMUNITY RELATIONSHIPS

COMMUNITY RELATIONSHIPS

We must behold the Lord individually. There is no substitute for individual intimacy with God. You can't delegate intimacy and the experiential knowing of the Lord for yourself. You must develop something with God and build your own history with Him. There is no way around this. This is because there is a beholding of the Lord that can only happen for us when we behold Him for ourselves.

But just as that is true, there is a beholding of the Lord that can only happen when our lives are knit together to others. Our lives being knit together is what God uses to create a habitation for Himself by His own Spirit at work in us and in the midst of us.[107]

Being knit together to others is a way to speak about relationships. God is relational. He is a divine family, a divine community. Out of that relational dynamic He has chosen to relate to us and reveal Himself to us. It is important

Our reference point for relationships must be God Himself and not our culture.

to Him that our lives are built together in relationship.

We miss out if we do not recognize God's grace in the place of relationships. Much of our culture has become so individualized in the way that things are considered. We mustn't allow this perspective or pattern for life to create a resistance to being a recipient of God's mercy, grace, and power in the place of community and relationships. Our reference point for relationships must be God Himself and not our culture.

God saves people to make them a part of a people. The Father has promised His Son a people. He is going to make good on this promise. The reward of Jesus' sufferings is a people, from every tribe, nation, and tongue.[108] This people that the Father has promised the Son is very important. This people are what

---

[107] See Eph 2:22
[108] See Dan 7:14; Rev 5:9; Rev 7:9

will produce the testimony of the Gospel throughout the world to every people group.[109] This people is not a peripheral issue; it is one of the reasons this age as we know it exists—for the Lamb to receive the reward of His sufferings.

We must recognize God's loving intentions for the relationships He desires. Through the relational dynamics and connections we are allowed and create, discipleship happens. Jesus said to go throughout the world and make disciples, teaching all people groups to obey everything that He has commanded.[110]

These are disciples, a people being conformed to the image of Jesus via the ongoing conditioning and cultivation of Jesus' value system in real time in real life.

We will touch on this in a greater way in the next chapter, but for now, we will suffice it to say that Jesus is looking for disciples. Not just converts or those who walk around claiming a mental or intellectual acknowledgement of His existence. Jesus is looking for a people whose lives have been powerfully transformed by the consistent harnessing of His Spirit bringing them into subjection to His leadership to do life His way.

---

[109] See Matt 24:14
[110] Matt 28:18-20

These are disciples, a people being conformed to the image of Jesus via the ongoing conditioning and cultivation of Jesus' value system in real time in real life. Another way to say this would be—discipleship: the consistent development of

The Church is not an event; the Church is a family.

learning how to do life Jesus' way.

Relationships are precious. Relationships can also be painful. Whatever our history with relationships, we have probably had a good dose of both precious and pain. If we have given our life to Jesus, relationships are unavoidable, and that is because the Church is unavoidable. Not the Church as an event, which is typically the way the Western version of the Church defines the Church—but the Church as a family.

There will be another place for this conversation, another book to come, but for now we will say simply and clearly that the Church is not an event; the Church is a family. And with the Church as a family, relationships are nonnegotiable for us. We must have one another.

There are fifty-eight "one another's" throughout the New Testament writings. The implications of what is being communicated is that we need one another to walk out and live well what the writers are communicating.

Relationships are necessary to the New Testament experience and the testimony that is being created for God Himself through this New Testament family of new creatures. This family of new creatures needs one another for the ongoing development of their own lives. We need the influence that comes off one another's lives as we live surrendered to Jesus.

Discipleship is about relational influence. We influence one another according to a certain way of life—Jesus' way of life. We are a Jesus people. The Father conforms us to the image of His Son.[111] The ongoing and increasing effect of this transformation happens through our lives continually bearing up under the work and process of discipleship.

We need the influence that comes off one another's lives as we live surrendered to Jesus.

As we relate to one another by our lives being knit together in real life, God works in us and in the midst of us on behalf of His own desires to have a people for His Son. Discipleship is key here, which is why relationships are key here, because relationships are one of the beautiful ways discipleship becomes real in our lives.

---

[111] Rom 8:29

Relationships are not easy. This is one of the reasons some choose to forego them altogether. They create excuses for themselves and exempt themselves from the necessary crucible God has for all of us in the place of relating to one another. Precious and pain are both possible in relationships. Some choose to go without the precious because of the sting and the trauma the pain can create. However, God has not changed His mind. He is committed to His way.

There are certain aspects and facets of our own transformation that require others to test or authenticate.

If we choose to live our lives without others, we will choose to resist elements of our own lives being conformed to the image of Jesus—because there are certain aspects and facets of our own transformation that require others to test or authenticate. There is something about relationships that reveal how much God has done or still must do as it pertains to our transformation.

The story of Cain and Abel provides us a great look into the power and potential that is to be had in the place of relationships. In Genesis chapter 4 we are given the story of two brothers. Cain is a farmer and Abel is a shepherd. Both seem to have a walk with the

Lord. We can conclude as much because the story tells of both brothers bringing an offering to the Lord.

The details are simple and very clear. God accepts Abel's offering. God does not accept Cain's offering. This scenario creates the controversy and the opportunity from which the story seems to be built. I say controversy and opportunity because most times there are opportunities in our controversies.

By rejecting Cain's offering, God doesn't shame him. In fact, we find God's grace and mercy to Cain in the instructions Cain is given about what to do. The Bible says Cain was angry when God didn't accept his offering. However, God reveals His heart in response to Cain's anger and it gives us a beautiful glimpse into the influence of relationships.

Most times there are opportunities in our controversies.

God says, "Why are you angry? And why is your face gloomy? If you do well, will your face not be cheerful? And if you do not do well, sin is lurking at your door; and its desire is for you, but you must master it."[112]

If you do well, won't your face be cheerful? Doing well is in direct relationship to learning from his brother. Abel's offering was accepted. Cain's offering

---

[112] Gen 4:6-7, NASB

was rejected. God's encouragement to Cain was to learn from his brother, who had already learned how to do well in relation to the offering that God desired.

God was encouraging Cain to glean from his brother's life and learn what it was that He desired. Cain was so infuriated with his brother that he decided to rise and kill him in the field. Cain's choice was to kill his brother rather than be changed by his brother.

We can watch one another in real time as we each live out our yeses to the Lord.

God's grace is revealed to Cain in that He already provided for him an example in his life that he could learn from. Cain wasn't left out in the dark as to what God desired. Cain had a brother who was living in a way that pleased God and who was bringing God the offering that He wanted.

Cain might have felt rejected, but he didn't have to look far to find a solution for his offering. What he was bringing to God was not right, and he knew it. Cain knew that his way of living wasn't right; however, he also didn't want to learn from the life example of his brother that God said was right.

The way that Abel was living was meant to relationally influence Cain into and unto what was right, which is what God desired. It is the nature of relationships. We are to learn from one another. We can watch one another in real time as we each live out our yeses to the Lord. This is incredibly impactful, and it is meant to be that way. Cain didn't want to learn from Abel. He was enraged by Abel's life.

Although Abel's life was meant to call Cain higher, it brought him lower. It brought him lower because he chose to kill his brother rather than be properly confronted by and changed by his brother. The provoking of Abel's life was meant to transform Cain and raise his standard of living before God.

Relationships have a way of bringing us higher in the way we offer our lives to God. Cain refused this invitation. The constant tension of his brother's life rubbed him to the point where, rather than being broken by the tension of God's grace and yielding to Him, he broke the tension by getting rid of the relationship God was using as an instrument to challenge him and conform his life. It is hard to deal with this tension for long periods of time. Typically, one of these responses always ends up winning out.

Relationships have a way of bringing us higher in the way we offer our lives to God.

Do you recognize God's grace to you in the relationships He has given you? That is, if you have allowed the inclusion of others into your life. The one another's is nonnegotiable to the Lord. At times we cry out for something in private. We ask God to give us breakthrough in a certain area. We long for the Lord to answer the cry of our hearts by giving us grace and bringing us higher in relationship to how we offer our lives to Him.

Most times, we cry out for something and God answers by sending us someone.

This is not wrong at all, and in fact, I believe it is one of the ways God fulfills His desires for us—He places longing in our hearts that create requests in prayer. But what I've noticed in most instances when we are crying out for something is that God has a specific way He most often answers.

Most times, we cry out for something and God answers by sending us someone. It is His way. The knitting of our lives together is working for Him a purpose He has in producing a people for His Son.

Our lives bring discipleship to one another. When I am around other dads or husbands I constantly watch and learn. Sometimes I learn lessons that are very challenging for me because I see a living example of what I long to be more of or become better at as a dad or husband. Other times I am challenged because I am watching an example I hope to never recreate in my own experience. Whether positive or negative there is always a lesson to learn.

I am using just one example of how important relationships become in our overall development in the image of Jesus, but you can imagine the possibilities here are endless, and that is the point. There are endless ways our lives are meant to bring discipleship to one another.

The church is the crucible where God is forming a people, a compatible companion, a bride, for His Son. The church, not just theologically, abstractly, or even preferentially—as we live out a consumer-driven approach that treats the church like Amazon or the mall and only browses the selections most appealing to us, so we think—but as a family is where God is performing His desires of readying the people that His Son deserves.

We can behold the Lord in relationships because we get to see Him in others.

This family is made up of new creatures that are involved in an ongoing training effort in bringing their lives into greater subjection to Jesus as King and are learning to live life by His value system or His way. This family is allowing the Spirit to form a habitation for God through the knitting together of their lives. This requires relationships.

We can behold the Lord in relationships because we get to see Him in others. We can see the way God has given Himself to people and in return the way people have given themselves to Him. This is precious and it is priceless. The value of relationships cannot be quantified. There is not a dollar amount that you could ascribe.

The lessons learned, the grace acquired, and the instruction and impartation received are life-changing. This is the way it is supposed to be; it is the way God has designed it. We can see Him at work. We can glean from His work in others and allow that same work to accomplish its agenda in us. We find the potential and the power to be changed by being knit together with those who have been changed.

We find the potential and the power to be changed by being knit together with those who have been changed.

Paul said to the Corinthians, "Follow me, as I follow Him."[113] This is the essence of discipleship through relational influence. I have found Him. I know the way. Follow me; I'll take you there. Praise God for His work in others and His grace to bring others into our lives. We must be open to our lives influencing others and being influenced by others. Or to put it in the language of our discussion here, we must be open to being disciples and then discipling others.

---

[113] 1 Cor 11:1

Beholding the Lord in relationships is vital. God believes in it. How can I say something like that? God became a man. God, as a man, lived His life with others. His life that was lived with others created an undeniable influence that transformed those who were close, and even those who chose to stay at a distance. God's life, as a man, lived in relationship to others, discipled them, and gave them a glimpse into what the Father was like. People were able to behold God in the person of Jesus.

And so it is with us. We are now ambassadors; we are representatives.[114] These representatives now relate to one another in family-style relationships to bring real discipleship and continued transformation to one another's lives. As representatives, we reflect what has been revealed to us. This revealing and reflection is one of the things God uses to change our lives as we are relationally knit to one another. We must behold the Lord in relationships.

We must be open to being disciples and then discipling others.

These tools are important pieces of our discipleship journey. Being formed into the image of Jesus is something that is intentional and requires intentional

---

[114] 2 Cor 5:20

work. These tools are protective and provocative. They help to protect us from falling away from the way. Jesus said the gate is wide and the path is broad that leads to destruction, and that many would find it. As a remedy for this He encouraged us to enter through the narrow gate.[115]

The Word, worship, fasting, prayer, and community relationships hem us in and protect us from falling off the way.

These various ingredients for our discipleship journey protect us as we have set our hearts to remain steadfast upon the narrow road. The long life of obedience in a singular direction is assisted and enhanced by these precious tools. The Word, worship, fasting, prayer, and community relationships hem us in and protect us from falling off the way. However, they also help to provoke us to be and become everything God has for us along the way. They are meant to protect and provoke.

There are other things God will use and employ in our developmental process, for sure. These are just a few that must become foundational to help us build the right foundation for our lives as disciples.

These ingredients will help us to abide in the current of being a disciple of Jesus. This is important

---

[115] Matt 7:13

because the world is headed in a very different direction and has its own current. The world around us is intentionally and aggressively trying to bring discipleship to our lives. Without these ingredients and tools, it becomes very difficult to know which way is which. But God has not left us alone in our efforts. The abiding power of the Holy Spirit within us consistently helps us to discern and illuminate the path.

CHAPTER NINE

THE PATTERN OF THE WORLD

The nations of the world are on a particular trajectory. They are all heading a certain way. There is a pattern that this age has formed, and the rulers of the age are attempting to conform everyone to its system. All the nations are included. The intensity of said influence will intensify as we draw closer to the end of the age.

Before Jesus returns the nations will rage in a demonic unity, with a hostility towards God, His Son as the chosen ruler of the creation, and those who have pledged their allegiance to Jesus as King and His ways. The devil and demon forces will recognize their time to be short and will do everything within their current experienced jurisdiction to influence the course of the world in a desired direction.

BEHOLDING & BECOMING

The influence of this attempt now is great, but it is not as great and the plan is not as outright as it will be in the closing season of history as we know it. May our hearts be conditioned to be ready for those days as they draw in upon us. May God give grace for those who will be trusted to participate.

America is not exempt from the raging of the nations. I live in the West, America, so I am more familiar with what is happening here than I am other nations of the world. Though I know certain things to be true of all nations because of what the Scriptures communicate, there are certain things that are very real to me because my life is sown in the soil of this nation contending for God's purposes in this hour of history.

America has a very real pattern. Paul, in his exhortation to believers in Rome, encouraged them not to conform to the pattern of this age.[116] This was to believers. This wasn't to those who are considered "separate" from Christ.

It is expected of those who have not yet repented of the world's system, renounced their inherent desire to rule over their own lives, and then pledged their allegiance to Jesus as King, to fall into alignment with the sin-saturated culture that surrounds. Meaning you expect those who are not yet alive to God and

---

[116] Rom 12:2

possessed by His Spirit to be caught in the current of the world—the sway of the wicked one.

There is a cultural current in America. There is a pattern, and it wants to influence everyone to join in and head the same direction as the push. John lets us know that the whole world is under the sway of the wicked one.[117] America is not exempt from the sway. The sway is the current, it is the pattern, it is the trajectory of the world, the system of the age. It is all synonymous.

It is important that we understand what is taking place so in our hearts and minds we can resist the discipleship agenda that has been launched.

The rulers of the age have launched an all-out war against God's loving intentions for His creation and want to disciple people to fall in line with their agenda, or to put it another way, be conformed to their image. It is important that we understand what is taking place so in our hearts and minds we can resist the discipleship agenda that has been launched.

We are not to be disciples of this world. God's goal is not to make you more worldly. At times we enter compromise by thinking that worldliness is relevance. It is not. God does not need you to be more like them

---

[117] 1 John 5:19

to reach them. That is not His master plan. His master plan is to make you more like His Son, which is wildly different than what the world trys to produce.

Being like Jesus is not supposed to be compatible with the system of the age. In fact, being conformed to the image of Jesus is going to be provoking to the world. It will either provoke them to repent and turn from their sins and the system of the world, or it will provoke the world to hostility.

Being like Jesus is not supposed to be compatible with the system of the age.

But being conformed to the image of Jesus, which is God's predestined goal for those that come to believe, is not neutral, and it is not intended to be. The sooner we realize that in our hearts, the sooner we can bear up under God's grace for the confrontation that being a transformed Spirit person is meant to produce. We are not of this world. We are not to be considered "normal" to them.

What is normal to the world are those that have fallen into agreement and alignment with the pattern. The current is heading in a desired direction, and the system appreciates, applauds, celebrates, endorses, and promotes those who have become participants and spokespersons for its way. Those who champion what the world champions and help to further its cause or current get elevated and esteemed.

There is an agenda, a discipleship agenda the system of the world is after, and the world will embrace and love as one of its own any who will help to facilitate and perpetuate that cause. All its causes, movements, rallying points, change efforts, indoctrination attempts, ways of evolving, and desires for transformation of culture should be seen for what is really happening. The world wants to disciple you. America wants to disciple you. The rulers of the age and the powers over America want you to get pulled into the current, the sway.

What discipleship agenda? Great question. The world wants you to remain one of its own. We are born into the world and until we repent of our sins, turn to Jesus, and have a born-again experience, we remain entrenched in the world and its system. We are prisoners of its lusts. The lusts of the flesh. The lusts of the eyes. The pride of life.[118] These are the governors. The discipleship agenda is fueled by the system of the age, which is built on the overindulgence of the lustful thoughts of the flesh and the mind.[119]

This agenda to disciple people is manifested in a variety of ways but is very targeted. The utter casting off of restraint, which is found through God's loving leadership, is the goal. Remove God, His ways, the

[118] 1 John 2:16
[119] See Eph 2:1-3

absolute truth of His Word, and the boundaries for the experiences of life that it creates.

Consider the sway America has been in. Many things have aggressively risen to the surface of our life experience and culture that we must discern. The deconstruction of the family unit and family values altogether. This has been taking place through the LGBTQ agenda and all their indoctrination efforts throughout culture with a very real emphasis on younger people and kids especially; through abortion; through our current supposed government assistance efforts and welfare; gender identity confusions and issues; and more.

The demasculinization and demoralization of male figures and their roles. The desire to normalize pedophilia by creating actual medical and scientific verbiage that attempts to diagnose people as being "minor attracted" as an actual condition. The goal of lowering the age of sexual consent in certain states to better legalize the attraction to young people, and by doing so also remove any criminal activity and penalty that may be associated with sexually engaging minors. The normalizing of violence and the degrading of women through music, movies, videos, social media content, and video games.

There is the constant use of political affiliation to subdivide people into categories and then breed

THE PATTERN OF THE WORLD

hostility and violence through said categories toward others that oppose. Racial tensions and racism that is propagated for gain—power, influence, and financial interests. The sexualization of culture cannot be ignored. The sexualization of culture that fuels the porn industry—which America is the leader of funding when compared to all other nations. The attempt to legalize prostitution and sex trafficking.

There is a rage building toward all that choose to not join ranks and help to push the proposed current.

These are several other items we can consider. Most of these have come rushing to the surface of culture within the last generation. Not to say that they are new, but the energy associated with them to normalize them throughout culture is very different than it has ever been. And it is progressing at an alarming rate. There seems to be an aggressive agreement being rallied. There is a rage building toward all that choose to not join ranks and help to push the proposed current.

Mainstream media agendas are in cahoots with all these items and help by wielding opinions and narratives that are in favor for whatever direction the current is flowing. Social media censoring and big tech affiliates have joined in also. Hollywood and the music industry have joined forces with the current and in many ways help to endorse and push forward many of the agenda items.

It is an all-out war. The intentions have been revealed. There is a direction that culture is pushing. There is a definition of success that the world and specifically America have created for what a successful life is supposed to look like. I am most familiar with America, although I am sure there are similarities for other nations.

The world considers successful those who have conformed to its push; the discipleship effort presently creating the current. We mustn't be too quick to forget that some things never change. The idea of normalizing things through culture using media, images, and music is not a new tactic. In fact, Nebuchadnezzar had the same plan.

Nebuchadnezzar had his plan of erecting a statue of himself; some translations use the word image. It was then to be accompanied by instruments or sound; let's say music. Through images and music Nebuchadnezzar realized he could wield his agenda of normalizing bowing.[120] Let's say it this way: the attempt to disciple a generation came through the constant use of images and music.

---

[120] See Dan 3

Nebuchadnezzar had a goal. The goal was not to entertain people with what was seen and heard. The overall goal was to get them to conform and to bow. Normalizing conformity and bowing was the destination, and the constant use of images and music was the pathway to travel to arrive at the desired destination.

There were also penalties for those who would not bow. A lack of conformity will always be problematic and will be met with brute force and pressure tactics. Conformity of the masses is the goal. The heat of the furnace will be ready for those who do not want to bow.

Normalizing conformity and bowing was the destination, and the constant use of images and music was the pathway to travel to arrive at the desired destination.

Against the demands of Nebuchadnezzar and the penalty of the furnace, we are told there are three Hebrew boys who didn't get down like everyone else. They chose to enter the furnace rather than entering compromise. As they enter the furnace, God reveals Himself as the One who draws near and stands with them in the moment of their trials.[121]

---

[121] Dan 3:25

He is not distant or unaware. He is very involved with those who allow the culture of the Kingdom to bring proper legislation to the matters of their hearts. Know this; there will be things found to be normal in culture that are not normal for those who are a part of God's Kingdom. Which is why we must be discerning of the current of the world, repent, and come out.

There will be things found to be normal in culture that are not normal for those who are a part of God's Kingdom.

Can you see it? Have you ever stopped to consider what is happening? Do you pretend it is not real and will all one day end on its own? Let me help you—it won't. The rulers of the age will not quit. Powers and principalities will not relent. It is why we desperately need salt and light. It is why it is necessary to have a city on a hill.[122] The need for bright stars that shine in a dark night sky is great.[123]

We must have those who have come out from among them and are now separate.[124] We must have disciples of Jesus, a radically transformed people, who are now representatives that can preach the Gospel with love and power to a broken people and offer them

---

[122] Matt 5:13-16
[123] Phil 2:15
[124] 2 Cor 6:17

repentance. It is the only way. The announcement of the Gospel must come to every nation, every region, every city, every people group, every tribe, nation, and tongue.

What does "come out and be separate" look like? Gospel 101 sounds like this: I have been born again—which means I have repented of my sins, laid down my entire life, and pledged my allegiance to Jesus as King. Now my life is not my own. Jesus is King, I am His subject, or bondslave, and what matters to Him is now what matters to me.

> **We must have disciples of Jesus who are now representatives that can preach the Gospel with love and power to a broken people and offer them repentance.**

I am not living for the system of the age or the American Dream, but I am an ambassador of God's Kingdom, a living representative of Jesus Christ, and He has become my dream. My ultimate delight is now found in being lovingly obedient to the One that has gone on before me and laid down His life for me, thus, now enabling me to live the life I don't deserve. He is mine and I am His. I have been joyfully conquered!

Belonging to Jesus means that His opinion is what matters most to me. I will stand before Him at the end of the age, and He will be the only One that has the right to validate the efforts of my life. This should really matter to us. The consideration that we will all face Jesus with the consequences of eternity should be sobering to us.

We will see Him. He will have something to say. What He says will be in relation to how we lived our lives. It will be the most important conversation we have ever had. We should all live considering the desire to hear, "Well done, My good and faithful servant."[125]

The definition of what a successful life looks like belongs to Jesus now.

Your life is not yours anymore. You belong to Jesus. This means that the definition of what a successful life looks like belongs to Jesus now also. It doesn't belong to you. It no longer is to be found in the world. Jesus, and loving obedience to Jesus, now determine what successful living means.

This may be tough, especially when we are constantly bombarded by the world's attempt to make us its disciple. The world aggressively presses you to believe what it believes, act like it wants you to act, and define the overall success of your life in the way it has prescribed to you is a success story. But you do not belong to the world, which means you should no longer define the success of your life by its standards

---

[125] See Matt 25:21

and goals. This is a hard pill to swallow, but we must swallow it.

David pens beautiful words when he says, "So teach us to number our days, that we may present to You a heart of wisdom."[126] David understood that God had a purpose to time. Time is a tool that serves a very real purpose God has. God is not subjected to time, meaning time is not His master. Time is a servant. It helps to facilitate the eternal longing God has in presenting to His Son a bride, a people compatible to Him and suitable to serve alongside Him forever as His beloved inheritance.

You do not belong to the world, which means you should no longer define the success of your life by its standards and goals.

David knew time was up to something. Because of this he knew he had to turn to the Lord to find out what real wisdom looked like. David realized God had a purpose for time, and because of that only God would be able to tell him what would be the right way to set up his life. David wanted to live the way God said was real wisdom.

At times, what God says is wisdom will be very contradictory to what the world says. But we must

---

[126] Ps 90:12, NASB

take note that the world is on a very different course. What the world says is wisdom will in many ways be in line with its agenda. The world measures success differently than God does. It is something we must constantly keep in mind as we travel through this life.

We too are like the great exiles of Hebrews chapter 11 who sought after a city whose builder and maker was God.

We too are like the great exiles of Hebrews chapter 11 who sought after a city whose builder and maker was God.[127] They realized this current world, meaning the sin-saturated system of the age and the jurisdiction of the rulers of the age, was not their home, and it is no more ours than it was theirs.

We are not setting our lives up to obey the world's commands. Before He laid down His life Jesus said, "Those that love Me will obey my commands."[128] After He was raised from the dead, He said, "Go, therefore, and make disciples of all the nations, baptizing them in the name of the Father and the Son and the Holy Spirit, teaching them to follow all that I commanded you; and behold, I am with you always, to the end of the age."[129]

---

[127] See Heb 11:8-16
[128] John 14:15
[129] Matt 28:19-20, NASB

Setting our lives up to honor Jesus, allowing the harness of His words and value system to overtake our lives, and the continual investment to condition our lives to obey His commands, is what we would call discipleship. This is our goal.

We want to be real disciples of Jesus. We want to live in a way that honors Him and His words. We want His values to shape our lives. We want all our life to be conditioned upon what He says is best. His definition of success is now what governs our existence. His voice, and the guidance of His voice, are what fuels all our dreams and endeavors. Our purpose is found in joy-filled obedience to the One we have given our lives to. We are known as those who have been joyfully conquered!

We are known as those who have been joyfully conquered!

Therefore, it is a must that our attention be drawn to how we can behold the Lord and receive His influence unto our continual transformation through beholding. We must give our heart's attention to Him and be continually influenced by Him so we are able to curb the influence of the world in our hearts to not become its disciple. The Word, worship, fasting and praying, and community are some of the beautiful tools we have as believers to condition our hearts and ready our lives in an ongoing way to bring to God a heart of wisdom.

The world's wisdom is irrelevant. It should no longer dominate our thoughts or dreams. If this is not the case, there will be many sticking points along the way where the way God is leading us or seeking to conform us will be halted by the consideration of what the world says or how we personally feel about what is happening.

We must be given over to God's influence and allow His influence to form every area of our life.

We must be given over to God's influence and allow His influence to form every area of our life. If we want to bring Him a heart of wisdom, meaning live our life in a way God says is truly wise, then we must come to Him, receive from Him, and let what we receive have its way in us so we are able to set up our whole life in relation to what we know God wants. He gives grace to accomplish His agenda. He will have what He wants.

CHAPTER TEN

AWAKENING THE GROAN

The world is broken. Sin has saturated all of life and created a system that is not at all what God originally intended for His creation. The effects of sin are real. We shouldn't look around and assume this is some new thing. It is a very old thing. The effects of sin have plagued man and the quality of his existence since the compromise in the garden.

Even during the days of Noah, we are told that every inclination of man's heart was always only evil. Jesus said that in the day He returns it will be as in the days of Noah.[130] Evil has filled man's heart, and therefore is filling the earth.

You don't have to look far to realize that things are not right. Darkness abounds. Corruption is celebrated. Injustice is on the rise. People are calling what

---

[130] Luke 17:26; Matt 24:37

is good evil, and what is evil good.[131] It is very easy to feel like Habakkuk did as he cried out to God.

In the first chapter of Habakkuk, we are told that Habakkuk was surveying the landscape of their situation. He didn't like what he saw. He wondered where God could be amidst all the unfolding drama and crisis that surrounded them. He was confused, because what he saw didn't line up with all the assumptions he formed about God.

Have you ever looked around and thought to yourself, *God, where in the world are You?*

Habakkuk cries out, "How long, O LORD, will I call for help, and You will not hear? I cry out to You, 'Violence!' Yet You do not save. Why do You make me see iniquity, and cause me to look on wickedness? Yes, destruction and violence are before me; Strife exists and contention arises. Therefore, the law is ignored, and justice is never upheld. For the wicked surround the righteous; therefore justice comes out perverted."[132]

Ever been there? Have you ever looked around and thought to yourself, *God, where in the world are You? What are You doing right now? Why is what You are doing or how You are doing it not directly confronting*

---

[131] See Isa 5:20
[132] Hab 1:2-4, NASB1995

and dealing with all of the cruel and painful things we must bear? If you have never been there, I have. And I am positive many others have been also. This is a legitimate question that fills the heart.

When injustice is running rampart. When the wicked thrive in the land. When perversion is celebrated, marketed, and a mockery of God has been erected throughout the land, our hearts groan. Out of this groan we seek the Lord. We seek Him because we know He has the power to make right all of what we currently look upon and experience that is not right.

The world is broken. We are planted right in the middle of the brokenness and the tension. The tension is not only on the outside, meaning out there somewhere in life, but it is also on the inside. The tension fills our heart. The tension we experience in life, of having to look upon what is not right, all the while being convinced that God will fulfill His dream and make things right, is what creates the tension.

We cannot be okay with the way things are because we understand things are not the way God ultimately desires.

We cannot be okay with the way things are because we understand things are not the way God ultimately desires—which is what makes it not right. It is not right, and we cannot be all right, because everything has not yet been reconciled to its right order.

We could never be okay with the way things are because the effects of sin and the jurisdiction of the rulers still exist. No matter how right things might look or feel for you, it is not right, and you should not be all right, because God has not made everything right the way He dreams of and will accomplish on that great day that He releases His Son to return, riding upon the cloud.

However much the dream of God may currently seem to be derailed to you, God will come; He will do as He promised.

However much the dream of God may currently seem to be derailed to you, God will come; He will do as He promised. He will bring an ultimate salvation and reconcile all things unto the leadership of His Son as the Ruler of the cosmos. The brokenness will be dealt with. The effects and influence of sin will be evicted. The wicked one himself will be eternally cast out.

The Lamb will be among of us.[133] He will fill all things. His bride will be with Him, ruling in glory as His companion. Forever will have begun. This will be a glorious day. Until then there is a groan that exists.

---

[133] See Rev 21:3-4

The groan is fueled by the knowledge of what we know is coming but are not living in the fullness of now. There is the tension of the now and not yet.

Solomon, after his quest for the meaning of life, came to a beautiful conclusion. In Ecclesiastes chapter 3 he writes a statement that seems so simple as we glance over it but is incredibly profound in the impact it creates in our hearts and has upon our lives. Solomon tells us that God Himself has put eternity in the hearts of men.[134]

Man carries a sense of forever. God has placed a branding upon the heart of man that causes him to realize there is more than just the immediacy of the bubble we live in. We are made for much more than just feeling like prisoners to the immediate. The immediate as we know it will one day fade. This age will pass.

We are made for much more than just feeling like prisoners to the immediate.

We will experience the end of the age one of two ways: we will open our eyes in the place of forever, eternity, having been raised from the dead; or we will be alive at the time of His appearing and be lifted to meet Him in the cloud of His coming.[135]

---

[134] Ecc 3:11, NKJV
[135] 1 Thess 4:17

There are a million ways to die. There are only two ways to be raised. Either we will be raised from the dead in Christ, or not in Christ. The options here are only two. Man's existence can be defined by all sorts of things while he is alive. There are plenty of categories that get created to place people into compartments so we can better know how to relate to them. However, at the end, when time fades and the King reigns supreme above every other, there will only be two categories. In Christ, or not in Christ.

There are a million ways to die. There are only two ways to be raised. Either we will be raised from the dead in Christ, or not in Christ.

I plead with you not to wait until He comes to find out which of these categories you are in. God has put eternity in the heart of man. You don't have to wait until then. If there is any question or doubt within you as to which category your life fits into, you can choose now to give your life to Him.

We know this is not all there is. We know there is more. And there is. There is so much more. And Solomon writes about man's heart being branded by God. But remember, this was an Old Testament passage; only to say that the Spirit had not yet been poured out. The Spirit being poured out has greatly intensified things. Now, we house the life of God on the inside, like a great treasure in an earthen vessel, and it creates a groan on the inside that cannot be avoided.

We are not to think it strange that we know things are not right. We are not alone in this feeling. The Bible tells us that even creation recognizes things are not right. Creation is groaning because it realizes it has been subjected to corruption.[136] The devastating effects of sin have produced a reality within creation that even creation knows is not ultimately what God desires. Creation is longing, crying out, groaning.[137] Creation groans for its day of salvation.

Creation longs for the reconciliation that awaits us all. Creation is living in a tension that can only be satisfied in one way— the King must come and take His rightful place. The sons and daughters of God must be revealed. Only the return of Jesus will satisfy the groan that exists in creation.

Only the return of Jesus will satisfy the groan that exists in creation.

Creation anxiously awaits the return of Jesus to make right all of what is not right. The alleviation of the burden will only come by the King coming. This is no small matter. Jesus must take His place. The

---

[136] Rom 8:20-21
[137] Rom 8:22

enthroned One must set up His throne in Jerusalem to rule the cosmos. He will free creation from its subjection to corruption and reconcile everything to a loving obedience to His Father's righteousness.

Creation awaits the revealing of the sons and daughters of God.[138] Creation waits for the suitable helper, the comparable companion, the bride the Father will fashion out of His desire to give His Son what He promised Him. Even creation knows that the Son, King Jesus, will rule alongside of a people. This people will be who help Him to steward the creation His Father has made.

He will free creation from its subjection to corruption and reconcile everything to a loving obedience to His Father's righteousness.

Creation waits for something very specific to be revealed. Jesus' inheritance is what creation anxiously longs to have revealed. Creation knows that once this people are revealed, the release will take place and the reconciliation will occur. The groan is very real. The groan erupting from creation is in alignment with what creation knows the Father desires. Creation knows the Father has a purpose and its groan is synchronized with that purpose.

---

[138] Rom 8:19

166

A few verses later in Romans Paul tells us there is another groan. This time it is not creation, but it is we too that bear the firstfruits of the Spirit that groan. The groan is produced from the tension of eagerly awaiting the fulness of our adoption, the redemption of our bodies.[139] We will be

We will be changed. We will be transformed forever. We will be eternal humans. This is the mystery of the resurrection.

changed. We will be transformed forever. We will be eternal humans. This is the mystery of the resurrection.[140]

Paul says in his first letter to the believers in Corinth, "Now I say this, brethren, that flesh and blood cannot inherit the kingdom of God; nor does the perishable inherit the imperishable. Behold, I tell you a mystery; we will not all sleep, but we will all be changed, in a moment, in the twinkling of an eye, at the last trumpet; for the trumpet will sound, and the dead will be raised imperishable, and we will be changed. For this perishable must put on the imperishable, and this mortal must put on immortality. But when this perishable will have put on the imperishable, and this mortal will have put on immortality, then

---

[139] Rom 8:23
[140] See 1 Cor 15

will come about the saying that is written, 'DEATH IS SWALLOWED UP IN VICTORY. O DEATH, WHERE IS YOUR VICTORY? O DEATH, WHERE IS YOUR STING?' The sting of death is sin, and the power of sin is the law; but thanks be to God, who gives us the victory through our Lord Jesus Christ."[141]

God's desire for a people to be with His Son forever will be accomplished. Nothing can defeat what God has set into motion through the cross of Christ. He will have what He wants. The resurrection is part of it. It must take place. Death, being the final enemy, will be abolished. There will be no more sting. Death will be as a tool in the hand of God—no longer ultimately destroying you, but now what God uses to transform you.[142]

Death will be as a tool in the hand of God— no longer ultimately destroying you, but now what God uses to transform you.

You will be changed. Our earthly bodies are planted in the ground when we die, but they will be raised to live forever. Our bodies are buried in brokenness, but they will be raised in glory. They are buried in weakness, but they will be raised in strength. They

---

[141] 1 Cor 15:50-57, NASB1995
[142] Samuel Whitefield, *Son of Man: The Gospel of Daniel 7, Vol 1*, (Grandview, MO: One King Publishing, 2019), 227.

are buried as natural human bodies, but they will be raised as spiritual bodies. For just as there are natural bodies, there are also spiritual bodies.[143]

There is only one thing that can satisfy the groan that fills the heart and life of the believer—it is God Himself and the manifesting of His purposes as He has purposed.

Paul says that we who house the Holy Spirit are groaning for this reality. We know this is reality, and our hearts burn for it. There are many things those who are of the world groan for. Wealth, fame, prominence, power, influence, a certain type of lifestyle, and more. But our groaning is not for things this life can satisfy.

No house will ever be big enough. No car will ever be nice enough. No number of followers will ever be able to fill the gap from within that houses the groan for God and His purposes. Like creation, there is only one thing that can satisfy the groan that fills the heart and life of the believer—it is God Himself and the manifesting of His purposes as He has purposed. This is it.

Until God gets what He wants and all things are made right, we groan. Our hearts are ablaze and our spirits are vexed. This groan has bubbled up from

---

[143] 1 Cor 15:42-44

within us and it has become us. For indeed in this house we groan, longing to be clothed with our dwelling from heaven, since we, having put it on, will not be found naked. For indeed while we are in this tent, we groan, being burdened, because we do not want to be unclothed but to be clothed, so that what is mortal will be swallowed up by life.[144]

Until God gets what He wants and all things are made right, we groan.

So far there is a groan in creation, and there is also a groan within the life of the believer. But there is one more groan I would like for you to take note of. The Spirit also groans. Paul says in Romans that within the life of the believer the Spirit groans. "Now in the same way the Spirit also helps our weakness; for we do not know what to pray for as we should, but the Spirit Himself intercedes for us with groanings too deep for words; and He who searches the heart knows what the mind of the Spirit is, because He intercedes for the saints according to the will of God."[145]

The Spirit on the inside of you is helping you. The Spirit is especially helping you when you do not know how or what to pray. The Spirit is interceding for you, from within you, because He knows what the perfect

[144] 1 Cor 15:2-4
[145] Rom 8:26-27, NASB

will of the Father is, and the groan produced by the Spirit, through intercession for you that is rising from within you, is in perfect alignment with what is on the Father's heart. The Father's will is in fact the same thing as His purpose, what He has purposed to do. This cannot be overlooked.

The Spirit within you is groaning and praying for you what God wants. This is to be especially taken into great consideration since the next verse is the very familiar, "And we know that God causes all things to work together for good to those who love God, to those who are called according to His purpose. For those whom He foreknew, He also predestined to become conformed to the image of His Son, so that He would be the firstborn among many brothers and sisters; and these whom He predestined, He also called; and these He called, He also justified; and these whom He justified, He also glorified."[146]

The groan produced by the Spirit is in perfect alignment with what is on the Father's heart.

Many get caught up on the language of predestination, but let us allow Paul to say exactly what he is saying, and that is, those who have come to believe have all been predestined to be conformed to the image

---

[146] Rom 8:28-30, NASB

of Jesus. The Father wants a people to look like Jesus, a people that are compatible to Him so they can be the suitable helper for Him.

The Father will use anything and everything to conform you to the image of His Son.

This is the goal of our predestination. The Spirit wants for you what the Father wants for you. The Father wants you to be conformed to the image of His Son. The Father knows this is good. He is working all things together for what He says is good.

Have you ever stopped to look at this verse? It's funny that some have added the emphasis of He is working all things together for your good. It does not say that. That would presume that what you think is good is what the Father thinks is good. This is not the case. The Father has already determined what is good—His eternal purpose, the dream of His heart, the eternal longing. His will is good. He wants a people for His Son. He longs to reconcile all things unto the leadership of His Son as he rules the creation from His throne in Jerusalem. This is what He knows is good.

He is working all things together for this purpose. There are many things that will happen along the way that you do not think feels good, looks good, or sounds good. The Father will use anything and everything to conform you to the image of His Son. All things will work together for what God says is good—for Him to have everything He is after.

There will be difficult processes and hard-to-interpret outcomes you experience that will all be part of a master plan the Father is weaving together as He superintends time and leads history towards His destination that He says is good. It is here that the Spirit prays. It is here that the Spirit groans.

The groaning of the Spirit in us and for us is to keep our lives synchronized with God's will. This is what Paul says the Spirit is praying for, because at times we do not know how to pray as we ought. At times our hearts are more prone to pray for things that we think are good; things that we think feel good; outcomes that we, by our own evaluation, have determined would be right. The Spirit helps us in our weakness.

The groaning of the Spirit in us and for us is to keep our lives synchronized with God's will.

Our weakness is that we don't always know how to pray as we ought. There is a mighty fountain, a river of life, on the inside that continually bubbles up and springs forth with intercession for the purposes of God to be accomplished. Accomplished in our own heart and life. Accomplished through us as we give ourselves to God and all He calls us to. Accomplished throughout the world as God works on behalf of His purpose, His will, to harvest for His Son the inheritance He deserves.

God is faithful beyond our understanding. He has given us His own life to secure for Himself the outcome He desires. It is not up to us alone, for we would have no shot. God has shared Himself with those who have given their lives to Him. He abides on the inside. His life, by His Spirit, is transforming us, conforming us to the image of His Son, and readying us for the day of His return.

God has given us His own life to secure for Himself the outcome He desires.

We are the people that Jesus will come to possess for Himself. We are His inheritance from every tribe, nation, and tongue. He will have a people for Himself, just as His Father promised Him. Until He comes, we groan.

CHAPTER ELEVEN

LOVERS INTO LABORERS

G od is going to give His Son an inheritance from every people throughout the world. Every tribe, every nation, every tongue. It may seem like mission impossible, and that's okay, God is not cowering away from the promise He gave His Son just because the odds are stacked against Him. He is going to be faithful to answer the heart cry of Jesus out of John 17, "Father, I desire that they also whom You gave Me may be with Me where I am, that they may behold My glory which You have given Me; for You loved Me before the foundation of the world."[147]

> **God is going to give His Son an inheritance from every people throughout the world.**

---

[147] John 17:24, NKJV

Jesus is crying out for the reward of His suffering—the people that His Father promised Him; the bride that He deserves; His inheritance from every people throughout the world. Jesus knows what He deserves. His Father will give it to Him.

Until Jesus returns the window of opportunity for repentance is open.

We are living in a window of great grace and mercy. Until Jesus returns the window of opportunity for repentance is open. What do I mean? There will come a moment when the sign of the Son of Man will appear in the sky. His Father will release Him from the heavens for His glorious and triumphant return. He will come riding on the cloud. He will come with a host of angels in all the glory and authority of His Father.[148] He will come for what His Father promised Him. The bride will have made herself ready.[149]

He will come with His reward for those who loved Him, lived for Him, and honored Him with the entirety of their lives. He will also come to recompense men for the deeds they did while they had time in the flesh. He will execute the judgment and eviction of the rulers of the age. This will happen at the end of time.

---

[148] Matt 16:27, NASB
[149] See Rev 19:7

Until we come to the end of time, we still have time. I know that sounds simple, but we must understand how critical the implications are. It is still day and we have time to work His works. Night will come and then no man will have time remaining to work.[150]

It is easy to look around and think that God must not care about all that is happening throughout the world. His perceived lack of interest is what causes Him to be distant and disconnected from all that is happening in our current events. When things are not going the way we think they should it is easy to bring this evaluation against God. However, Peter gives us a little bit of insight and helps us to better understand what is really happening.

Until we come to the end of time, we still have time.

Peter, in his second letter, brings a much-needed exhortation about the last days. One of the ways he describes those days is to say that there will be a dominant theme, men will be given over to their own lustful desires.[151] Their fleshly cravings will dominate their lives. Out of that he says people will become mockers at the consideration of the return of the Lord. The return of Jesus will become a joke, and people will literally mock others for the very thought of it.

---

[150] John 9:4
[151] 2 Peter 3:3

It is here that he says, "But do not let this one fact escape your notice, beloved, that with the Lord one day is like a thousand years, and a thousand years like one day. The Lord is not slow about His promise, as some count slowness, but is patient toward you, not willing for any to perish, but for all to come to repentance."[152]

Do you realize that if Jesus returned right this moment there would be no more time left?

God is not slow. He is patient; He is kind; He is long-suffering. He is long-suffering out of a desire He has. He desires that all would come to repentance. He doesn't want any to perish. This is His heart. This is the eternal longing—God wants a family, a people He can share Himself with forever.

Do you realize that if Jesus returned right this moment there would be no more time left? Let this thought really hit your heart. There would be no more time. With the return of Jesus comes the end of the age. Time as we know it on this side of life will cease. Death, the final enemy, will be abolished forever.

For some, they will enter eternity to be His comparable companion. But that means there will be no more time. No more time to make changes. No more

---

[152] 2 Peter 3:8-9, NASB

time to yield to Him in a greater way. No more time to cultivate a greater love for Him in your heart. No more time, period.

Why does this matter? It matters because the return of Jesus will also mean there is no more time to repent. No more time to repent. There will not be any more time, because time will cease. Those who are not right with God will no longer have time to become right with Him. Those who have not bowed their knee and pledged their allegiance to Jesus as King will no longer have the chance to do so willingly.

I say that because at the end of the age every knee will bow and every tongue will confess that Jesus Christ is King to the glory of God the Father.[153] But at the close of time, at the sign of the Son of Man time will end, and with it the window of opportunity will close and a finality to the age will be experienced.

Have the implications of the return of Jesus really hit your heart? Have you really considered that His appearing will be what the prophets declared as the great and terrible day of the Lord?[154] It will be great for some. It will be terrible for others. It all depends on what happened while there was still time for it to happen.

---

[153] Phil 2:9-10
[154] Joel 2:31; Mal 4:5

God's desire is that none would perish. He doesn't want anyone to choose hell as an eternal fate. Who would choose hell as an eternal fate? The one who doesn't choose Jesus, that's who. The one who wants to rule over his or her own life, be their own God, reject the idea that there is a loving Creator who is God and has laid down the pathway to eternal life through the blood of His own Son as the rightful ruler of creation. That's who chooses hell. We must remember that hell was not primarily created for people, but for demonic forces rebelling against God and His desires.[155]

We must care more for people's eternal condition rather than their momentary emotional condition.

We must allow the eternal implications of this thought to be as weighty as they are. We must stop trying to appease people's desires by making the situation more palatable for them. We must care more for people's eternal condition rather than their momentary emotional condition.

We want to be liked. We cater to the lie that we shouldn't offend people. All the while we are not living with the urgency required to bring the announcement of the Gospel to those who most need it. We are seeker

---

[155] See Rev 19; Rev 20; Jude 1:6

sensitive. We are mild, weak, and timid. All the while people are dying and will face Jesus and the consequence of eternity without having repented.

There will be people that were in your life on that great day when we all face the judgment seat of Jesus that will ask you why you never told them. They will ask you why you didn't preach the Gospel to them. While there was still time to do so, why didn't you announce His coming again to them so they could ready their heart?

This should be an incredibly sobering thought, and one we should not take lightly, brush off, and keep living our lives as we always have. This thought requires an alteration. May God give us grace to make the necessary changes while there is still time to do so.

May God give us grace to make the necessary changes while there is still time to do so.

At least for right now there is time, and God is gracious. He is gracious and understands very much so the consequences of the return of His Son. He longs to give His Son what He promised Him, and He will.

One of the ways He is working toward the conclusion He is committed to is by repopulating the nations of the world with His family of new creatures, those who are born again and are now a new creation. It is these ambassadors that He is scattering throughout the world. Every nation. Every city. Every people. These ambassadors are being planted in the soil of every place throughout the world to be representatives.

They are not living life for themselves, no. These ambassadors are consumed with a heavenly dream and are now living as faithful ambassadors, recognizing they carry a word and a ministry on their lives. Like Paul said, "All this is from God, who reconciled us to Himself through Christ and gave us the ministry of reconciliation: that God was reconciling the world to Himself in Christ, not counting men's trespasses against them. And He has committed to us the message of reconciliation. Therefore we are ambassadors for Christ, as though God were making His appeal through us. We implore you on behalf of Christ: Be reconciled to God."[156]

Paul recognized the born-again life also came with a word and ministry attached to it. The same grace that was extended to the one who considered himself to be the chief of sinners and then the least of the apostles realized the same way the window—to repent—had been opened to him was still open to others.[157] And while it was open to others, Paul wanted to maximize the opportunity at hand.

---

[156] 2 Cor 5:18-20, BSB
[157] See 1 Tim 1:15; 1 Cor 15:9

He says they were imploring men to be reconciled to God. Implore can be defined this way: to beg urgently. Let's input that into what Paul is saying here and read it again. As ambassadors for Christ, we urgently beg you to be reconciled to God while the window of opportunity is open and there is still time to repent. This changes our frame to understand what Paul was saying, and it needs to.

Paul saw fit to urgently beg people to be reconciled

> **As ambassadors for Christ, we urgently beg you to be reconciled to God while the window of opportunity is open and there is still time to repent.**

to God. Do you? Paul understood the implications of the return of Jesus, and it moved him to announce the Gospel with great urgency, even unto begging people to repent and be reconciled to God. Does the thought of the return of Jesus move you this way?

When I say beg people to be reconciled to God through repentance, what I am not saying is watering down the Gospel message through a seeker-sensitive approach to boost your Sunday attendance numbers. I am not saying that we should cater to the love of the world and for the sake of not offending people make repentance a bad word and allow people to claim a love for Jesus in any type of lifestyle they think is best.

Or because we desire people's money or influence, we don't lay down the cost of following Jesus because we seek to leverage what it is they bring to the table toward our mission and vision. I don't think any of these things were a part of Paul's intentions. We must let the consequence of eternity give us an immediate urgency that moves us to preach the Gospel while there is still time to do so.

We must let the consequence of eternity give us an immediate urgency that moves us to preach the Gospel while there is still time to do so.

Jesus said as you go, preach the Gospel of the Kingdom.[158] What is the Gospel of the Kingdom? If it is what we are supposed to preach it would be helpful that we understood what it is. We must know it if we are going to announce it to the peoples of the world that surround us.

The Gospel of the Kingdom is the announcement that there is a King who is going to return. He is going to take His rightful place. He will confront everything opposed to His love and leadership throughout creation. He will abolish death. He will right every wrong. He will deconstruct and do away with every kingdom that exists.

---

[158] See Matt 4:23; 9:35; 10:7; 24:14; Mark 1:15; 11:2; Luke 9:60

He will evict evil and the rulers of the age. He will possess a people for Himself from all the peoples of the earth. He will rule with His bride alongside Him. His throne will be physically established in Jerusalem and He will rule all the creation from there, forever.

This is the announcement of the Gospel of the Kingdom. This is the message all of creation must hear. It is the announcement of the Gospel of the Kingdom that provides men with the opportunity to repent and ready their hearts for the return of the King and His Kingdom. Is this what you are preaching?

The Gospel of the Kingdom is offensive. It is offensive because it declares to us that we are not God. Our desire to rule our own lives is confronted by the announcement of the Gospel. The Gospel demands that all men must repent to be reconciled with God. There is no other way.

God understands what He has done, and the way is the way. The way is repentance. Repent of your sins. Repent of your rebellious desire to rule your own life. Repent of your love of the world and the system of this age. Repent and be reconciled. This is the way.

Jesus said, "If any man would come after Me, he must first deny himself."[159] Why is it that most of us never make it to the place Jesus saw fit to begin,

---

[159] Matt 16:24

meaning self-denial? Self-denial is the doorway to Kingdom discipleship.

God is scattering His family of new creatures throughout the peoples of the earth to bring this Gospel announcement. They **God is turning lovers** will have their own lives **into laborers.** conformed to the image of Jesus to be readied for His second coming. They will help to ready the earth through the proclamation of the Gospel and the offering of repentance to men.

God is turning lovers into laborers. Those who love Him will now labor with and for Him. Those who love His Son and have given their lives to Him have now joined the mission that God is on. They are ambassadors of His cause. Their dream is His dream. Therefore, they will represent Him until He comes again.

This is an offering of mercy from God. The window is open. While it is open, He is doing all that He can to offer men the opportunity to repent. He is patient because He has a desire.

CHAPTER TWELVE

THE WILD ONES ARE RISING

A proper response to the Gospel begins with denying ourselves. If any man would come, let him first deny himself. This implies that my life is no longer my own. This means I have surrendered the whole of my life to Jesus as King. I now live as His representative. I am an ambassador for His Kingdom rule. My delight is in doing His will.

> **A proper response to the Gospel begins with denying ourselves.**

I love Him and so I will obey Him. His smile over the obedience of my life is what I desire. He has become my dream. All other attractive things this life once offered and appealed to me have faded. His radiance eclipses all the shine and sparkle of the world's enticements and entrapments.

Everything else I used to find significance in and identified by is now, and I believe Paul said it best—garbage.[160] There is now only One. This One outshines the rest; He is the chiefest among ten thousand.[161] I will live for Him. He is to die

Forever and always, it will be Jesus and Jesus only.

for. He has fully given Himself to me, therefore I have fully given myself over to Him. My life goal is to know Him and to make Him known. I want Him to be glorified in me by life or by death.[162] Forever and always, it will be Jesus and Jesus only.

God is raising up a people that will live their lives out of being totally smitten for Jesus. A tribe of wild ones that will be lovesick. Out of His current absence, the lives of these precious and powerful lovers will house a Maranatha groan. This groan will not be satisfied by worldly things. This people will live by God's wisdom. Their whole lives will find delight in His Law, His commands. They will be a fiery tribe who will abandon all other and lesser lovers. They will have concluded that He is worth it and give their all for and to Him.

---

[160] See Phil 3:7-9
[161] See Song 5:10, KJV
[162] See Phil 1:20

They will set their whole life up against Him and a belief in His reward at the end of the age for those who have been faithful. Against all the options and considerations of what and how to live they will choose to live their lives in response to the beauty and worth of Jesus.

God is raising up a people that will not think it to be excessive to live in response to the beauty and worth of His Son. They won't think of it as a chore. They won't see loving Jesus as an obligation to get what they really want, which is the retirement package the relationship offers. This won't be some dry religious obligation; they will be head over heels in love with Jesus. They will love Him for Him. He will be the object of their affections and the source of their delight.

> **God is raising up a people that will not think it to be excessive to live in response to the beauty and worth of His Son.**

This people won't consider it to be unrealistic that someone would choose Jesus and willingly and joyfully forsake all others considering the treasure that has been found in Him. For these wild ones, Jesus will be the ultimate obsession. God will have a people that believe His Son is worth it and will live like it. It will happen. It is happening.

There is a powerful prophetic declaration in the book of Malachi. Malachi declares that there is coming a day when God will have a people throughout the nations, from every people, that will live their lives in response to His beauty and worth. Listen to what Malachi says, "My name will be great among the nations, from the rising of the sun to its setting. Incense and pure offerings will be presented in my name in every place because my name will be great among the nations."[163]

God is going to have a people from every nation. This is His heart. He is going to see it all the way through.

Malachi erupts with this wild prophetic utterance. His words pierce through the impossible to shine a bright light on what is contained in God's heart. He releases this word, and with it comes a sword that cuts. The sword cuts all our preferences. The sword cuts all our perceptions. God is going to have a people from every nation. This is His heart. He is going to see it all the way through.

Malachi's words are still true. They ring loud and reverberate throughout the centuries of time. His word wasn't just a trendy or relevant fad; it was an eternal revelation, a word from the Lord. It doesn't matter

---

[163] Mal 1:11, CSB

how unrealistic this may seem to us. God is doing it, and He will accomplish it in full. Nothing will be missing. There will not be anything lacking. What He promised His Son, He will make good on. A people that will love Him from every nation, every people.

I know this creates some immediate complications in our heart as we consider how God could pull this off. We think this way because of the complexities of the global situation. There are nations that currently consider themselves to be post-Christian. There are others that are considered atheistic in orientation. Other nations are governed by radical ideologies that are incredibly hostile toward believers and the idea of Jesus altogether.

What the Father promised His Son, He will make good on. A people that will love Him from every nation, every people.

There are nations that are lukewarm in their approach to a faith or confession of allegiance. Then there are nations that are self-consumed and overtaken by their power and affluence. It is difficult to consider how God will do it when we survey the landscape of the nations.

Our hope doesn't lie in the news media. Our source of inspiration isn't found in the most popular talking head for whichever outlet or channel we prefer to be informed by. Social media is not our guide. None of these are where or what we are looking to regain traction with our confidence with the things that we know are ultimate. These sources shift and bend to whatever is most popular. Whatever currently sells. Whatever will get clicks, views, or follows.

Regardless of what we see, we know God is faithful and He will bring to fruition everything He has spoken.

No, our sourcing, like Habakkuk, is from above. We climb higher to wait to see what He will say. Here we can set down our anchor once again. Regardless of what we see, we know God is faithful and He will bring to fruition everything He has spoken. All His promises are yes and amen in Christ.[164] And He has made a promise that He will have a people for His Son from every people throughout the earth.

Every dark place where the Gospel is unwelcomed, God will have a people for His Son. In every closed-off nation where there is radical rejection to Jesus and the idea of His supremacy, God will have a people for His Son. In the most cold and calloused places, God will have a people for His Son. In the places where we think people don't deserve it, God will have a people for His Son.

---

[164] 2 Cor 1:20, NASB

Have you ever considered that God's promise to His Son is not limited by your preferences? God is going to redeem people from places where you might not prefer that He do so. Our likings are not at the heart of what shapes what God is doing throughout the nations. His promise to His Son is giving definition to the powerful work His Spirit is performing right now to bring that promise to pass.

Jesus deserves a bride. These wild ones will be wholly His. He deserves it. There is one man that can live with entitlement and be entitled to do so. It is right. He is right. He is the worthy One. He has overcome. He has purchased a people for God with His own blood.[165]

He has made a way to have the bride that He wants. This bridegroom King has left His heavenly home to come to the earth and cling to His bride. For a man shall leave his family and cling to his wife, and the two shall become one.[166] The two have now become one.

He has given us His Spirit. He has sent another to be with us.[167] He burns for union, oneness. The destiny that's been promised Him, the reward of His suffering, He must have it. His desire erupts from His heart as He prays openly for others to take notice

---

[165] Rev 5:9
[166] See Gen 2:24; Eph 5:31
[167] John 16:7

of what He longs for, "This people, I have to have them . . . they must be with Me where I am!"[168]

Until He comes these wild ones will live in response to His greatness. Malachi's words will be fulfilled. They are being fulfilled. There are a people emerging. The bride is taking her place on the stage of history. There is a shine, a radiance, gaining visibility. Like a bright star that is properly hung in place and shines in the dark night sky, the bride is making herself ready.[169]

Malachi says that incense and pure offerings will be made in response to God's greatness in every place throughout the nations. Let's make this simple. Incense is a reference to prayer and intercession.[170] Pure offerings can be understood as a reference to worship.[171] God will have a people who know they have access to Him and as an ongoing way of life will stand before Him, minister to Him, and bless His name. They will then, out of this life given over to ministering to Him through prayer, worship, and intercession, represent Him to their neighbors and nations.

These Levites will behold Him, and out of beholding Him will minister to Him day and night.[172] These Nazarites will answer the beckoning of the Spirit

---

[168] John 17:24
[169] See Phil 2:15; Rev 19:7
[170] See Rev 5:8
[171] See Gen 22:5
[172] See Deut 10:8-9

and give themselves over to God in a peculiar way.[173] They will abandon the other lovers of this life to be more given over to the One that they love. Their hearts will have been captured and they will joyfully be known as those who follow the Lamb.[174]

These Levites and Nazarites will live this way, not because they must, but out of a recognition that He is worth it. Their love for Him will be demonstrated by the way they set up their lives. They will love Him above all things, the way that He deserves. His Spirit in them will give them grace to give themselves to God in a way that may be viewed as uncommon. King Jesus will have conquered their hearts!

Jesus will be enthroned in the hearts of His people. He will be their King. They will live like it.

Jesus will be enthroned in the hearts of His people. He will be their King. They will live like it. It won't be the adoption of a new language or catchphrases. It won't be social media memes and little hashtags here and there. It won't be the trendiest Christian merchandise. It will be real.

Not to say that you cannot do these things and have it come from a place where the actual substance of it is being lived out in your life; you absolutely can.

---

173 See Num 6:1-2
174 Rev 14:4

But you also can use these other things while Jesus is not everything to you. He is going to become every thing to those that love Him.

The bride will be provoking because she will not sing the song of the nations or dance to the beat of the system of the age.

Out of Him becoming everything, those that love Him above all things, His bride, will worship Him. In worshipping Him, His bride will enthrone Him upon their praises.[175] As these wild ones turn from worshipping the vain idols and things of the world, His kingly rule will reign in their hearts as they worship Him and adore Him.

The bride will be a catalyst for spiritual awakening as we lean in closer to the end of the age. She will be provoking because she will not sing the song of the nations or dance to the beat of the system of the age. There will be a groan that brings her cry into perfect harmony with what the Spirit desires. There will be a synchronizing of the groan of the bride and the groan of the Spirit.

In the last days, the Spirit and the bride will say, "Come, Lord Jesus."[176] There will be a recognition that only one thing will do—Jesus must come. The

---

[175] See Ps 22:3
[176] Rev 22:17

heart of the bride will no longer be enamored with the world or worldly things—all the vain goals; all the fleshly ambitions.

All the self-manufactured and self-fueled dreams that were never born from God will come to an end. There will be a radical abandon. God will orchestrate and superintend events that see to it that the cry of the bride is severed from all other lovers. Fame. Fortune. Fascination with self. They will all lose their glisten. The bride will live for one thing, and this one thing will become her cry.

God will orchestrate and superintend events that see to it that the cry of the bride is severed from all other lovers.

The return of Jesus will come to the surface in the heart of the bride. The subject of the return of Jesus will fill the lips of intercessors. The return of Jesus will be declared from preachers. The return of Jesus and the sense of His reward for His faithful ones will take center stage.

It will be necessary. It will once again provide the much-needed fuel to the heart fire of the bride to come out of the world and be separate and honor that One she adores and awaits the imminent return of. These wild ones will be faithful to Him, and faithful to the very end.

The idea of being faithful to Him to the end is exactly what Gabriel communicated to Daniel, "But as for you, go your way to the end; then you will rest and rise for your allotted portion at the end of the age."[177]

You have the Holy Spirit; God will not abandon you to the grave.

These words close out the book of Daniel. These words provide the gauge as to how we are to consider faithful living for our own lives. "Go your way to the end." God has made it clear. The path has been set. The way is narrow. Do not come off it. Do not be deceived. Do not give way to enticement. Remain. Persevere. Stay strong. Finish well.

The encouragement is to the end. Not halfway— all the way. Not just three laps of a possible four, but all four laps. As Paul said, "I have fought the good fight, I have finished the course, I have kept the faith; in the future there is reserved for me the crown of righteousness, which the Lord, the righteous Judge, will award to me on that day; and not only to me, but also to all who have loved His appearing."[178]

"You will rest and rise." Even if you face the grave, God will come for you. Even if you die, God will be faithful to what He promised. Just as He raised Jesus,

---

[177] Dan 12:13, NASB
[178] 2 Tim 4:7-8, NASB

He will raise you too. You have the Holy Spirit; God will not abandon you to the grave.[179] You will be resurrected. You will rise at the end of the age. God will do it. He gave you His Spirit as a down payment pledge toward it. He will be faithful.

"Your allotted portion." There is a reward for those who love Him and live for Him. There is a portion exclusively for those who pledged their allegiance and chose to live in a way that honored their King. He will come. His reward will come with Him. It will be forever. There is not one who can alter what it is that He desires.

> **You will be resurrected. God gave you His Spirit as a down payment pledge toward it. He will be faithful.**

"At the end of the age." Time will end. All our lives will be judged. Jesus will be King forever and His justice will reign throughout. He will be the exalted One that will fill all things. Toward the end of John's revelatory encounter he says, "And I heard a loud voice from the throne, saying, 'Behold, the tabernacle of God is among the people, and He will dwell among them, and they shall be His people, and God Himself will be among them, and He will wipe away every tear from their eyes; and there will no longer be

---

[179] Ps 16:10

any death; there will no longer be any mourning, or crying, or pain; the first things have passed away.' "[180]

The prize always eclipses the pain.

This is what God wants, it is what He is after. The dream will have been realized.

Leonard Ravenhill is quoted as saying, "Are the things you are living for worth Christ dying for?"[181] Many times we have dreams we think are quality enough ideas to give our lives to them. But at the end of the day, is there really a cause that is worth your life?

I grew up as a military kid. I was surrounded by people that had made a vow to protect and preserve even at the cost of their very lives. This people were grafted into a cause they thought was worthy enough of a dream to give their life to see fulfilled if it came to that. They fully bought in and believed it was worth it. I am grateful for them, for sure. But what about you? Is there really a dream that is worthy of your life? I would suggest there is.

To answer the question correctly we must look away from the world and all its causes it supplies. We must investigate the face of God. We must behold the person of Jesus afresh. As we behold the person

---

[180] Rev 21:3-4, NASB

[181] *Good Reads,* "Leonard Ravenhill Quotes," https://www.goodreads.com/author/quotes/159020.Leonard_Ravenhill.

of Jesus again and again, we are confronted by a man that had a dream He knew was worthy of a life, and not just any life, as if that one life was better than any other, but the life of God Himself.

This life is greater in worth than every other. This dream was so extraordinary. This dream had enough weight to it that it moved God to do something about it to secure it. This dream had the price tag of a life attached to it, and God paid it in full with the payment of His own blood.

If you were to ask God, "What is the dream that moved You to give Your life for it?" I believe He would say to you, "A family." God is a family man. His eternal longing moved Him. The dream of giving His Son a bride to serve alongside Him as a suitable helper in the place of eternity set things in motion. The cost was great, but the thought of having the dream fulfilled outweighed it. The prize always eclipses the pain.

Do you think God's dream is worthy of your life? The way you live your life will answer the question.

The desire to give His Son what He promised Him, a family, is what moved God to do what no other could do. But what about you? Is what God wants enough for you? Do you think God's dream is worthy of your life? That is not a rhetorical question. It must be given an answer. Lip service will not suffice. The way you live your life will answer the question.

God is going to have a people that live in response to Him being great. These faithful laid-down lovers will give their lives in a great way to what God says is great—the great dream, the eternal longing! These lovers turned into laborers will give themselves to Him and His mission because what He wants will be what they want.

These lovers turned into laborers will give themselves to Him and His mission because what He wants will be what they want.

His groan will be their groan. His heart cry will be the cry that rises from their hearts. The entirety of their lives will be overcome by the joy of partnering with Him and seeing His dream accomplished.

God knows He will have a people throughout the world, in every place, that will live in response to His greatness. Through a life of beholding, they will become everything God desires for them. Their lives will be aligned to His heart. He will awaken the groan on the inside of them. They will be a people who house a groan for God and His purposes. They will be wild and will wildly give themselves over, empowered by God's grace.

Do you see your life here? Do you see your life in the context of God's story? Or are you still trying to figure out where God fits into your story? Let me help you. God is not trying to fit into your story. He has laid down His own life and now opened His life to you. The veil has been torn. He has let you into His life and created a place for you in His story. But that invitation requires a response.

How will you respond? What will you say to this great King? How will your life answer the heart cry of God? It is one thing to know what God wants. It is another thing to also want what God wants and be willing to give your life to it.

> It is one thing to know what God wants. It is another thing to also want what God wants and be willing to give your life to it.

At the end of your life there will be a Man. We will all stand before Him. He will have fire in His eyes. He will be the most loving Man we have ever encountered. He will also simultaneously be the most righteous and just Man we have ever encountered. One quality will not take away from the others; He will be all things in the most beautiful and consistent way.

He will have something to say about your life. His perspective and opinion on how you lived your life will be what matters most. It will determine your experience of eternity. We must ready our hearts and live our lives with this moment in mind. Not in fear, but out of holy love and jealousy.

I pray you will know what He wants, that you will be filled with the knowledge of His will. I pray that in being filled with the knowledge of His will you will walk worthy of the call. It is time.

Until He comes, may we groan for God and His purposes . . . Maranatha, come Lord Jesus!

Michael Dow

Michael Dow and his wife, Anna, have been married for fifteen years and they have five children together. Their family resides in Orlando, FL, where they lead a growing group of house churches called The Father's House. He is the cofounder and president of Burning Ones, an international ministry team helping people all over the world experience the love and power of Jesus and live more passionately devoted to Him. Michael is the author of several books, including, *Fasting: Rediscovering the Ancient Pathways*. Michael holds an undergraduate degree in theology from Southeastern University in Lakeland, FL, and travels the world preaching the Gospel with powerful signs and wonders following into gatherings of all kinds.

CONNECT WITH MICHAEL DOW

BECOME A PARTNER

BURNING ONES IS HELPING PEOPLE AROUND THE WORLD
EXPERIENCE THE LOVE AND POWER OF JESUS AND LIVE
PASSIONATELY DEVOTED TO HIM.

FOR MORE INFORMATION ON BECOMING A PARTNER
SCAN THE QR CODE BELOW OR VISIT:

BURNINGONES.ORG/DONATE

DOWNLOAD THE BURNING ONES APP
STAY UP TO DATE WITH ALL BURNING ONES NEWS

In the app you will have access to messages, worship, news and updates, the Bible, livestream events, and much more.

RESOURCES

FOR OTHER BOOKS, RESOURCES, AND MERCHANDISE
SCAN THE QR CODE BELOW TO VISIT THE
BURNING ONES ONLINE STORE.

CONNECT

CONNECT WITH BURNING ONES

@_burningones

@burningonesinternational

www.youtube.com/burningones

Info@BurningOnes.org

Burning Ones
PO Box 772610
Orlando, FL 32877